THRIVE WHERE YOU ARE
WHILE STRIVING TO GET WHERE YOU WANT

Introduction

Chapter 1 – From Surviving to Thriving

- Where Do You Start to Get Out of Survival Mode?
- Thriving Tools
- Thriving Points to Consider
- Additional Thriving Resources
- Thriving Prayer and Confession

Chapter 2 – Shifting Your Paradigm

- Thriving Tools
- Thriving Points to Consider
- Thriving Additional Resources
- Thriving Prayer and Confession

Chapter 3 – Thriving

- T – Tenacity
- H – Healing
- R – Reflection (Self)
- I – Imagination
- V - Vision
- E – Eliminate and Engage
- Thriving Tools
- Thriving Points to Consider
- Thriving Additional Resources
- Thriving Prayer and Confession

Chapter 4 – Starting Point

- No Limits No Excuses
- Be Content Where You Are
- Always strive for better
- Thriving Tools
- Thriving Points to Consider
- Thriving Additional Resources
- Thriving Prayer and Confession

Chapter 5 - Position Yourself

- Get your mind right
- Make sure your image is on point
- Get your hands on as much as you can
- Work hard, but more importantly work smart
- Thriving Tools
- Thriving Points to Consider
- Thriving Additional Resources
- Thriving Prayer and Confession

Chapter 6 – Attributes to Have While Thriving

- Office Etiquette
- Lead by example
- Don't Expect Praise or Appreciation from Anyone Other than God
- Operate in Character and Integrity
- Be Patient
- Thriving Tools
- Thriving Points to Consider
- Thriving Additional Resources
- Thriving Prayer and Confession

THRIVE WHERE YOU ARE
While Striving to Get Where You Want to Go

TERESA LANDRUM-CASWELL

Memphis, Tennessee

THRIVE WHERE YOU ARE
WHILE STRIVING TO GET
WHERE YOU WANT TO GO

Copyright 2015 © by TERESA LANDRUM-CASWELL

All rights to this publication are protected and recorded with the Library of Congress Washington, DC
All rights reserved under international copyright conventions. No part of the contents of this book may be reproduced or utilized in any form or by any means, electronic or mechanical, including photocopying, recording, or by any information storage and retrieval system, without the written permission of the author.

Cover Design
AVGP Media
Memphis, Tennessee

Production
Virtual Marketing & Publishing
Memphis, Tennessee

ISBN: 978-194384907-9

First Edition

Printed in the U.S.A.

Chapter 7 – Success: What It Really Means To You
- Give and Empower Others
- Thriving Tools
- Thriving Points to Consider
- Thriving Additional Resources
- Thriving Prayer and Confession

Chapter 8 - Balancing While Thriving
- Seek Help From Others
- Know Your Balance
- Eliminate the Feeling of Guilt
- Prioritize Accordingly
- Thriving Tools
- Thriving Points to Consider
- Thriving Additional Resources
- Thriving Prayer and Confession

Conclusion

About the Author

References

Counting our blessings in the present is the key to receiving God's abundance that is already there. Practice the attitude of gratitude.

ACKNOWLEDGMENTS

I am so thankful for the opportunity to share my story to inspire others. This is my purpose, my passion, and I am operating in my vision.

I want to first thank God, my King and Father for all the obstacles I have overcome by His grace and mercy. I know that I can't have a testimony without a test.

I want to thank my parents, Aljay and Lula Landrum, for always believing in me and displaying a Godly image before me and my siblings.

I want to thank my husband, Charlie Caswell, for being the great supportive, visionary God has called you to be. A loving father and a GROWING husband!

To all my children – Kiara, Tiara, Xzavia, Destiny, Charlie, and Autumn. You all inspire me beyond words. All of you are special and unique with certain attributes I see that will make you highly successful. My prayer for all of you has always been, "Father, I pray that they will respect themselves, others, and demand respect from others." I see my prayer being fulfilled on a daily basis and I know all of you will be highly successful.

To my siblings, Jason and Tamika, I know the best is yet to come. We have always challenged each other to be better (others may call it competing, but I call it challenge) and I know we will exceed indeed our parents' expectations.

To all my spiritual parents, past and present – Apostle and Deaconess Rogers, Apostle and Co-Pastor Sheila Floyd, and Pastor and First Lady Alice Smith. I thank all of you for your love and guidance to encourage me and help me grow into the person I am today.

Last, I dedicate this book to all women. Single mothers, married women, any woman who feels they don't have the drive or ambition to live up to the standards that society put on us as women. Nothing is impossible with God and we will walk in our purpose, passion, and vision.

INTRODUCTION

What is different from you and other women who are successful? What do they have that you don't possess? One major difference is those women believe in themselves. They have the drive, ambition, and are operating in their passion and purpose. They set goals and have a plan of action and when obstacles and barriers approach them, they have a "NO LIMIT, NO EXCUSE" attitude. They did the work. They went through the process. For other people to believe in you, you must first believe in yourself.

I have overcome many obstacles and I won't tell you I did it overnight. In fact, it took me many years to overcome the feeling of loss and what I felt like was failure. It took me a while to get back on my feet, but when I made my mind up, it didn't take me long. I know you have heard it many times but I want to remind you again. "It's not how you fall or even how hard you fall or how long you've been down, but it's about how you get back up."

I have evolved from a depressed, hopeless, visionless woman looking for love in all the wrong places to fill the void to a woman of joy, a loving and happy mother and wife. As a single mother on welfare, statistics show I should not have accomplished all that I've accomplished, BUT God. I have my MBA, insurance license, multiple certifications, entrepreneur drive, and a beautiful family. I have been praised for my accomplishments, but I knew there was something missing. It wasn't until I did a personal inventory of where I was and where I wanted to go that I began to see the potential and open doors that were available to me.

I don't want you to think I have it all together and I am done growing because I'm not. Every day I continue to challenge myself to become a better me, but I have grown and I use my obstacles as stepping stones taking it one step at a time and one day at a time. I consider myself to be highly successful. I'm not successful because I drive luxury cars or live in a luxury house. I consider myself successful because I walk in my purpose, I have vision, I serve God and his people!

Office administration has always been my passion. I'm good at it. I make it look easy and I love doing it. I have exceptional abilities to organize, analyze, and envision how things could operate better. I've always had a professional image that has left a lasting impression wherever I worked. However, office administration doesn't pay well in the positions I've obtained; therefore, I went outside my passion and purpose and did something that brought in more money. It wasn't until that moment I realized operating in your passion and gifts offers many rewards other than just compensation. If I am operating in my passion and purpose all the rewards will come. God will lead me, guide me, direct me and connect me with the right people to make those visions come to pass and what I consider FBI….FAVOR, BLESSINGS, AND INCREASE WILL FOLLOW!

I began to operate in my purpose by using social media to inspire women. I mentored single mothers in the Frayser community to inspire them and offer a helping hand. I assisted women with cover letters, resumes, and interview tips to position themselves in the workforce. I assisted non-profit organizations. It wasn't until I began to do this that I felt joy, fulfillment, and gratitude. I was operating in my purpose.

I encourage you to walk in your purpose utilizing your gifts. Put on the mindset of Christ and serve in whatever position you are in. Thrive where you are while positioning yourself to strive where you want to be.

This book will provide tools and resources to thrive where you are. The content is for women seeking to expand and evolve in their career and relationships. However, the principles and tools can also be applied to women who feel stuck, empty, and hopeless and need that extra push to get out of their comfort zone.

Something about you that I truly admire,
Words from your mouth often inspire.
Glass is half-full, you clearly see,
Your positivity brings joy to me.

You're a combination of special and rare,
So many talents, with the world you share.
Just the way you make others feel,
Is so wonderful, it's simply so real.

Wherever you go, whatever you seek,
I know you will conquer, no matter the peak.
By the look in your eyes, I can sense your drive,
I'm so happy, I know you will THRIVE!

~ AnitaPoems.com

CHAPTER 1
FROM SURVIVING TO THRIVING

I know about barely surviving. I moved to Memphis, TN with my daughter and a car full of things. No job. I had a place to stay but was told within a week I had to move out. As a single mother on welfare, I made up my mind that I no longer would love a man who didn't love himself or know how to treat a woman, but I would go through the work on myself and let God send me my husband.

I came to Memphis, got a job, got into church, laid before God's feet as much as I could. He transformed me from a clubbing woman into a worshiper. From a drunk into a server. From a fornicator into a wife. From a victim of abuse to victorious. It was then that I begin to thrive.

Surviving is all some people know, but when you get to know God who is all mighty and all powerful and you get to know his word… you will learn that he wants you to THRIVE. He wants you to be PROSPEROUS. If you begin to seek God where you are… He will take you where He wants you to be – walking in overflow and abundance.

That which we obtain too easily, we esteem too lightly. ~ Thomas Paine

I've learned things that are handed to you are not appreciated as much as things you have had to work for. I look at people who have money handed to them from a family legacy and they blow through it because they don't appreciate it. They didn't work for it. Look at the people who win the lottery. Statistics show that within a five year period, the majority are broke again. Why? Because there is no blood, sweat or tears behind the money they received.

When you've gone from welfare to making over $50,000/year through your hard work, dedication, commitment, and God's help, you learn to appreciate it. You can't tell God thank you enough. You lay at His feet with tears flowing down your face saying, "God, I surrender to you." You learn to manage your $ better. You learn to appreciate how far you have come. You learn to trust God through the good and the bad.

There were times when I was operating in survival mode. I didn't have enough to pay the bills or get the necessities. I was robbing Peter to pay Paul, then it went to both Peter and Paul were broke! What do you do then? You go through the process!

Where do you start to get out of survival mode?

Recently my children and I were on the highway going to Illinois and we were going through a terrible storm. God began to show me some things. At first, all the children were asleep, but then my 14 year old heard me praying and she popped up and stayed awake with me. I have gone through a lot of storms and for every single one of them my 14 year old has always been right there with me by my side through them all. I call her "my ride or die." Also, my youngest ones have never known we were going through the storm just as they didn't this time…they were in the back seat asleep.

When you are with God, children will follow your lead. There are all kinds of "storms." I remember when our lights got cut off and we stayed in the hotel. My husband, I, and my 14 year old knew the situation, but the little ones were happy to be staying in a hotel.

As we were going through that storm God said, "Often times people give up during the storm or they pull over to wait for the storm to pass, but not you. You always keep going. You may slow down, but you never give up. You pray your way through." I said, "YES and God you have always been faithful to bring me out." God then said, "Look in your rear view mirror, look at what you just came out of." I looked and I saw dark clouds and people pulling over stopping. I began to praise him for bringing me and my family out of the storm. He said "Now look ahead….what do you see now?" I looked ahead and I saw the sun shining bright! Never give up during a storm. Slow down if you must, but pray your way through. Keep looking ahead…don't look back. Get to your destination. Soon you will see the sun shining bright. Give God the glory and Praise!

    We will all have storms to go through, but God will be right there with you to bring you out. It is so easy to get depressed by focusing on all the problems we have before us, but I want to remind you, there are things in your life that you can be grateful for. Think about those things. Don't focus on the problem, but focus on solutions. If you can't see a solution, then focus on what God has already brought you out of and trust Him to bring you out of this one. Focusing on the problems will only lead to you feeling overwhelmed, hopeless, and depressed. Focusing on solutions will lead to you being optimistic about the future. Take on the mindset to see every problem and obstacle as an opportunity to grow and evolve and use what you have. The more areas you have problems in, the more areas of opportunity you have to grow in. When you change your mindset to focusing on solutions rather than your problems, you will begin to attract opportunities because that is where your focus and energy are. You have everything you need right now to start the process.

    When I started writing this book, all I used was the notepad in my phone as God began to give me chapters. Every night He would give me a different chapter and give me the right words to say. I didn't fret "I don't have a publisher" or "I don't have a laptop"…no I started with what I had and let God lead me from there.

Believe that you are where you are now and this is preparation for your future. Often times what we see as a demotion is actually a promotion. I love Oprah Winfrey and I have read about her journey. She was molested at age nine and gave birth to a child at 14 who died in infancy. At age 19 she became the youngest black woman and first news anchor and was promoted at age 22. Then she began receiving negative comments about being dull and stiff and mispronouncing words. She was then "demoted" to a failing talk show. Oprah did not take this as a demotion. At the time she was devastated, but now as she (and we) look back we see this was clearly a promotion. What did she do? She used the resources she had and started to thrive where she was.

If you want to know where your focus and energy is look at your daily habits. Scroll through your Facebook page and see your post in the last week. Are your posts inspiring to others or are they negative? Are they more focused on family or reality shows. Look through your checkbook. Are your clubbing expenses more than your tithes? Did you pay your tithes? Can God trust you with more because you are faithful over a little? Are you ready for another vehicle or is your oil light on in your current car? Begin to prepare your mind to stop surviving. Quit living day to day and begin to think about your future.

The very first thing is that you must have a relationship with God. Paul explains, "And we know that in all things God works for the good of those who love him, who have been called according to his purpose." (*New International Version, Rom 12:2)*. This verse explains you must have a relationship with God … you must love God and He will work everything out for your good. God will use what you consider misery into your ministry. Your ministry means "serving God's people." Also, the Bible says, "Instead of your shame you will receive a double portion, and instead of disgrace you will rejoice in your inheritance. And so you will inherit a double portion in your land, and everlasting joy will be yours". (*New International Version, Isaiah 61:7*). Therefore, whatever trials you went through…not only will He turn it around for your good, but He will also give you double for your trouble.

  Second, it is important to evaluate where you are now and see your future and believe in yourself! Know your worth and know your value! Know that you have unique attributes that only you possess and the world is waiting for it. Even if other individuals or businesses are doing what you do, only you can do what you are called to do in the way you are called to do it. For example, I know many people can do resumes, but only I can use my gift of writing and administration to make a person who works at McDonalds look like a person who has great customer service skills with the ability to work in a Fortune 500 company! Other people may be able to do it, but nobody can do it like me. That is the confidence I have and that is how I believe in myself! I applaud other people's unique gifts, but I also believe in mine as well.

  Third, ask yourself, "Do I have vision?" Vision is the source and hope of life, so if you are feeling hopeless, 9 times out of 10, you don't have vision. That is the #1 starting point. (We will touch more on vision later in the book.)

  Fourth, ask yourself, "Am I walking in my purpose?" Purpose is what you do to inspire others. Purpose is about making a difference in the lives of others. Purpose is about using your strengths to serve others while bringing yourself joy.

Fifth, find out who is for you and ask for their guidance. Surround yourself with positive people. ELIMINATE TO ELEVATE! Get rid of toxic people and things that will keep you bound. Find a way to make your situation better. If you are lacking education, enroll in school. If you are lacking a job, dust off your resume, get it professionally done (I can help you with that), seek guidance on interview tips, step up your professional image, and start somewhere.

Sixth, find a daily time where you meditate, pray, do confessions to speak positive circumstances into your life so you can attract positive things. Definitely commit to a church that will strengthen you spiritually and find a place to serve.

Seventh, operate in resilience. You will experience challenges and roadblocks anytime you try to change a pattern. This is where resilience kicks in. You have to be able to bounce back. This is something that you will develop over a period of time. You have to adopt the mindset that "this is just one of many challenges I will overcome." You have to work through each challenge to have a testimony.

The point is GO THROUGH THE PROCESS. I had to apply these steps also. As I stated before, I was on welfare and I applied the steps. I don't see anything wrong with using the system to get on your feet. That is why it is there. However, the problem is when you become reliant on the system and you are not going through the process while you are on welfare. I was in an abusive relationship and I had to go through the healing process. I lost cars and houses and I had to go through the rebuilding process. I know God has the power to turn everything to work for my good.

I know God ALLOWED (not created the problem but allowed) me to have financial problems so He could show me how much of a provider He is. I know God ALLOWED me to lose cars and houses so He could show me how much of a redeemer and restorer He is. I know God ALLOWED me to be in an abusive relationship so He could show me how big of a healer He is. I know God ALLOWED me to go through all that so I could tell my story and encourage others. Go through the process to make a future better for you and your children, to leave a legacy for your grandchildren, encourage and motivate others, and to become a person that is Thriving! Remember, our failures are not final and our mistakes are not fatal.

If you fail, never give up because F.A.I.L. means
"FIRST ATTEMPT IN LEARNING"

End is not the end, in fact E.N.D. means
"EFFORT NEVER DIES"

If you get No as an answer, Remember N.O. means
"NEXT OPPORTUNITY"

SO LET'S BE POSITIVE

~A.P.J. Abdul Kalam

Thriving Tools:
1. Evaluate your relationship with God. Do you have a relationship with Him that expresses your love for Him?
2. Evaluate where you are today and where you want to go as well as the steps you need to take to get there.

3. Believe in Yourself. You have unique gifts that the world is waiting on, but in order for people to see the gift you have to see them first.
4. *Do I have vision?* If the answer is yes, then consider what is hindering the vision. If the answer is no, continue to read more on Vision in Chapter 3.
5. Am I walking in my purpose? What are your strengths and how can you use your strengths to enhance and inspire someone else?
6. Find a daily time to pray, meditate, speak confessions, and visualize where you want to be in life.
7. Begin to pinpoint people and things that are toxic and go through the elimination process.
8. Be resilient. When faced with challenges, bounce back stronger than what you were before. Use that challenge to grow from, learn from, and excel from.

Thriving Points to Consider:

What do you consider your misery?

What is important to you today? (Look through your social media pages and banking accounts.)

What are your unique gifts God blessed you with that the world is waiting on?

Who/what are some people in your life that are toxic that you need to eliminate to elevate?

When is your designated time you will spend with God each day?

Who are some positive, supportive people you will surround yourself with to encourage growth and development?

Where can you start today – enroll in school, start looking for a job?

Thriving Additional Resources:

Download You Version app on your phone (free app) and download some daily devotionals such as Joyce Meyer, Rick Warren, and Joel Osteen. Also, download a daily Bible reading plan to begin to fill your heart and mind with the Word.

Thriving Prayer:

God, I thank you for your grace and mercy. God I thank you for giving me strength to go through the process to make life better for me, my family, and others around me. God, I thank you for connecting with me a great support system to help me go through the process. I know you say in your Word "you wish above all that I prosper and be in good health" and now I stand on that Word wishing the same for me as well. I know nothing is too hard with you for you are King of Kings, Lord of Lords, Almighty and All Powerful. Help me to be more selective about everything and everyone who has my ear and the people I allow to influence my life as I go through this process. Holy Spirit empower me, inspire me, and motivate me to grow into the woman you have called me to be. Bless my hands to be diligent and not self-indulgent and bless everything I put my hands to. I am ready to begin the process. Let's go. In Jesus Name!

Thriving Confession:

I choose today to begin the process. I choose to get out of the process of survival mode to thriving. I will be successful. I will leave a legacy for my children and grandchildren. I will inspire and motivate those around me. I will use my hands to serve others and use my tongue only to speak positive words. I am operating in wisdom in my career, business, relationships, family, and finances. My future looks bright and successful. I declare this in Jesus Name!

Moving Forward

What a moment you have brought me to
Such a freedom I have found in you
You're the healer who makes all things new.

I'm not going back, I'm moving ahead
Here to declare to you my past is over in you
All things are made new, surrendered my life to Christ
I'm moving forward.

You have risen with all power in Your hands
You have given me a second chance.

I'm not going back, I'm moving ahead
Here to declare to You my past is over in you
All things are made new, surrendered my life to Christ
I'm moving forward.

~ Israel Houghton (Edited)

CHAPTER 2
SHIFTING YOUR PARADIGM

Private victories precede public victories and making and keeping promises to ourselves precedes making and keeping promises to others. ~ Stephen R. Covey

Breaking Generational Curses

When you are going through the process to thrive, you will need to recognize deep problems that have evolved from generation to generation. It is during this time you have to realize how deeply imbedded and rooted your perceptions are. During this time we have to look at the lens through which we see the world and determine what influences could be in our perception. That will help us understand how and why we see the world the way we do.

Sometimes we see things a certain way because that was how our parents always saw it. Therefore that is what was imbedded in you. I remember a story about a daughter who asked her mom, "Why do you always put the turkey in the pan that way?" The mother replied, "This is how my mother always did it so this is how I do it." So the daughter went and asked her grandmother, "Why do you always put your turkey in the pan like that and now my mama does the same thing?" The grandmother replied, "I did it that way because at that time, all I had was a small pan and couldn't afford anything bigger...I don't know why your mama does it that way."

This story is an example of how things we saw our parents do can affect why we do things a certain way. During this phase of thriving, we must realize that if want to change the situation and break the curse, we must change ourselves first. That also means changing our perception - change the lens through which we currently see the world.

In the book, "7 Habits of Highly Effective People" by Stephen R. Covey, he talks about the paradigm shift, the way we see the world – not in the terms of our visual sense of sight, but in terms of perceiving, understanding, and interpreting.

Author Stephen Covey used two different maps as an example to explain paradigms: a map of way things are (realities) and a map of the way things should be (values). Without the right map, you will become frustrated and angry trying to reach your destination. You can have the right behavior, but you will only reach the wrong destination faster. You can have the right attitude. You still may not reach your destination, but you would not think negative about it. To try to change outward attitudes and behavior is useless unless we examine and research the basic paradigms from which our attitudes and behaviors flow. Every time you speak to describe what you see, you are describing yourself, your perception, your paradigm. (Covey, pg. 316)

You have to start with yourself. Begin to look at your paradigms, character, and actions and the motivation behind your actions. Author Cohen explains "private victories precede public victories and making and keeping promises to ourselves precedes making and keeping promises to others." If we begin to work on the outward before exploring and working on the inner, we set ourselves up for failure. Yes, it may work for a short period of time, but to have a lasting effect, we have to explore from within. This can be a painful process, but it is a rewarding process.

One example, people think women who are on welfare are lazy. Yes that is the case in some situations, but not always. After hearing several of the women's stories, many of them can't do better because they don't know better.

Many of them are doing what they saw their parents do, operate in survival mode. Therefore that is what they are doing. To them, it is a way of life. It's a generational curse. This is what is imbedded into them.

The system is set up to have women comfortably living on the system. If a woman has free rent, free food, free daycare, free health insurance, and the option to get help on light a bill, that is preferable. Because going out getting a job for $8.00/hour with only a high school education, then having to pay daycare for four children, buy food for four children because food stamps are reduced, and now the option to get help on her light bill is no longer available (or reduced) because she has a job, which option sounds more comfortable?

Also how the system is setup enables fathers to stay out of the homes because federal housing does not want the father on the premises. That leaves more "fatherless daughters" which leads to girls who have no respect for themselves looking for love in all the wrong places which leads to teen pregnancies. And the cycle continues.

My goal in providing this example is to get you to see things from a different lens. Why is it that you have that perception of women on welfare?

One example I have of something that was embedded into me that motivated me to look at things through a different lens is the marriage my father and mother portrayed before me. Yes, my parents are successful and they have been married for 40 years, but times have changed from when they got married. My parents both retired from Caterpillar and were considered "middle class." They both worked the "8-5" job to provide for their family. We went on yearly vacations, lived in a nice house in a nice neighborhood, attended nice schools (predominately white.) Consequently, my sister, brother and I all received college degrees. I considered this to be comfortable.

That is what I wanted out of my marriage – steady income, monthly budget, living comfortably. However, when God connected me with an entrepreneur, visionary, go getter man with no education who was raised in a single family home, the belief I had on what I thought marriage was SUPPOSED to be quickly faded. We didn't see things the same way. We had different family values and beliefs. I had to look at things from a different lens to see that all marriages will not be like my parents and that's okay. I didn't know how to handle adversity in a marriage because I didn't ever see my parents go through adversity.

Now, as an adult, I realize my mother had a strong, entrepreneurial spirit. I didn't know about entrepreneurship when I was younger because I didn't notice it in my parents' pursuits. I wasn't aware of multiple streams of income because it didn't register with me. In fact, growing up in a certain religious denomination, I was told (not from my parents) that having a lot of money was considered a sin. Then, after I began to read and research on my own, I learned "the love of money is a sin," but not having multiple streams of income. In fact, I've learned it is mandatory in today's economy to have multiple streams of income.

It wasn't until that moment I realized I had to do the work: Educate myself on marriage. A marriage where God calls you to serve and walk in vision and purpose because we know the stronger the calling, the greater the anointing, the more challenges we will go through. Educate myself on entrepreneurship, rich vs. wealth, love of money vs. love to make money.

My husband and I went through counseling, prayed, and went through the process. We still have many adversities, but now, I don't think something is wrong with our marriage because it doesn't look like how I thought it was supposed to look. It looks like how God wanted it to be – a marriage focused on Godly principles with purpose, passion, vision, and serving.

Although my parents are successful, I don't remember them receiving debt free cars and giving away debt free cars. I don't remember them writing a book or running non-profit organizations to serve the community. I had to realize God has a strong calling on our lives; therefore, we must walk in faith and trust Him through the process.

Thriving Tools:
1. Recognize deep problems that have evolved from generation to generation and go through the process to end the cycle.
2. Work on yourself first. Pinpoint attributes and traits that are not healthy and beneficial to you that may be holding you back from thriving.
3. Recognize some beliefs and values that have been embedded in you that you may need to look through a different lens to thrive.

Thriving Points to Consider:

What are some beliefs and values that have been imbedded in you that you may need to look through a different lens to THRIVE?

How can you begin to start the process of educating yourself to change your paradigm from the lens you currently see?

Thriving Additional Resources:
- Romans 8:28
- Isaiah 61:7
- Book – *7 Habits of Highly Effective People* by Stephen R. Covey

Thriving Prayer:

God, I thank you that you have opened my eyes to see some things I need to change the lens from which I see things. I thank you that all generational curses are broken and the cycle stops here! I thank you that I am THRIVING in every area of my life because I choose to do the work and go through the process. I thank you for giving me the strength and courage to work on the inner me. I know this can be a painful process, but I know it will be a rewarding process. I want to walk in the goodness and likeness of you. I know all things are possible with you on my side. Reveal to me the areas I need to change and give me patience as I know this will be not be done overnight. In Jesus name I pray. Amen!

Thriving Confession:

I am joint heirs with God therefore I reap the abundance of the royal life laid down before me. My children are blessed, my grandchildren are blessed, and I am a blessing to others. We are walking in overflow and abundance. I am thriving in every area of my life. Great things are in store for me. I have favor, blessings, and increase following me. I am the head and not the tail, above and not beneath; victorious, righteous, and prosperous. Every generational curse is broken. The cycle stops with me. In Jesus Name!

Get Focused – let go of the need to feel important.

We are a part of a culture that thrives on feeling important through busyness.

We live in a society that chases money and fame.

We have a crazy need to be popular.

This is a trap that keeps us striving instead of thriving.

~ **Unknown**

Money and recognition are just by-products of the true wealth in our lives... that we are all richly blessed children at One with God.

CHAPTER 3
THRIVING

SURVIVING is IMPORTANT; THRIVING is ELEGANT
~ Maya Angelou

Webster defines thrive as:

Verb – To prosper in any business; to have increase or success. To increase in bulk or stature; to grow vigorously or luxuriantly, as a plant; flourish; as, young cattle thrive in rich pastures; trees thrive in good soil. **Synonyms: flourish, prosper, get ahead, expand, boom, gain in wealth.**

When I think of thrive, I think of:

- T – Tenacity
- H – Healing
- R – Reflection (Self)
- I – Imagination
- V – Vision
- E – Eliminate and Engage

All of the words listed above are verbs or attributes needed to thrive where you are.

Tenacity

To thrive, you must be willing to endure adversity with strong determination. Anytime you seek to prosper, adversity will come. You will have haters and obstacles you have to overcome. You have to have your mind made up that change begins with you and you are willing to go through the fire to thrive. You must be determined.

Anytime you think of a successful person, they had to endure adversity. Most millionaires will tell you that it took three or four times to get that game changer idea or business. They had to be persistent, tenacious and endure adversity. My favorite scriptures when it comes to tenacity are:

- ***I can do all things through Christ that strengthens in me. (NIV: Philippians 4:13)***
- ***Greater is he that is in me than he that is in the world. (NIV: 1 John 4:4)***

What will get you through adversity? Prayer, faith, mediation, and confession in the spiritual realm and passion, drive, and ambition in the natural realm. Will it be easy? NO. Will it be worth it? YES!

My sister in law, Vanessa Caswell Rodgers, is one of the most tenacious people I know. She has overcome many obstacles, but the important word is that she has *overcome*. She went to the doctor and received a bad report and she made up her mind that her health mattered. In addition, she chose herself over a relationship that was not healthy for her, Now, she is happily married, healthy, and serving others in her Organization, "Annie's Scale Back" (before and after pictures in the appendix.) When I asked her, "What does tenacity mean to you?" she said:

> ***Tenacity is the quality displayed by someone who just won't quit, who keeps trying until they reach their goal.***
>
> ***I fall greatly in this zone due to struggling with poor health, bad relationships and recently had the zeal to being an overcomer. Let's start out with health issues and being overweight all my life. On December 10, 2010, I was told by my physician***

that my sugar level, cholesterol and blood pressure were high and I could not afford to gain another pound standing at 317. She stated she would give me until March 2011 to lose some weight or she would have to add insulin and cholesterol medication to my daily regimen. I was already taking 3 high blood pressure medications.

She then reminded me that my body does not belong to me, but it belongs to the Lord and she began praying with me. On that day, I made a commitment to take authority over my health. The next morning, I woke up and went into prayer myself, stepped on the treadmill and at that point I was walking 2-3 miles everyday. I also altered my portion intake, sugar intake, carbohydrate intake and changed my meat selections to turkey, fish and chicken. When June 2011 came, I was down 64.4 pounds.

I continued on until I was at an 80 pound weight loss and during October 2012, I began to gain weight due to depression regarding getting bad news of my mother's failing health. My mom went through her illness for 6 months and as of May 11, 2012 she passed away putting me into a deeper depression and again finding comfort in food.

I then had to go evaluate myself again because I had put 30 pounds back on after that. Going back to my physician and her giving me the same lecture January 2014 and me sharing with her the hurt of losing my mother, I had to find comfort and it was found in snacking, no exercise and loading my plate.

She had to remind me that my body didn't belong to me and to go to God in prayer for comfort and that by me overeating would only put me in an early grave like my mom. She encouraged me to turn the hurt around and get healthy again and make my mom proud of me. Well I must say that as of April 2014 I took the authority back and through constant prayer and determination, I'm the smallest and healthiest I've ever been.

Another obstacle was being in a 7 year relationship, being promised a lot of hope, happiness and marriage that never came to pass. Being told that I wasn't his soul mate and to move on put me at another determined state. I promised myself that I was and am a PROVERBS WOMAN and I had a desire to be a wife and I would wait on the Lord and get Vanessa out of the way. With fasting and much praying, I was delivered from that relationship and 8 months afterwards, the Lord blessed me with my Boaz. So, I say in all things, put Christ first, love yourself and thank him for your storms.

It's easy to keep going when things are going good, but the real test is when you can't see the ending. When you are going through the storm and yet you keep driving knowing eventually you will be there. You don't see the destination with your natural eye, but you see the destination in your mind and in your heart.

Healing

To thrive, you have to go through the healing process. Healing often times means forgiveness. Unforgiveness doesn't affect anyone but yourself. It holds you back from reaching your full potential. Unforgiveness is a sickness that continues to grow and often times is contagious. You must go through the healing process before you plan to grow. Do whatever you have to do to bring healing to yourself so you can grow and THRIVE.

When I think of a woman who went through the healing process, I think of my Best Friend, Gyvonne Williams. She had many adversities; two miscarriages and one failed marriage that really hurt her. She was bitter, angry, a MAD BLACK WOMAN. Now she is happily married with two boys, serving in the ministry, and just bought a new house. I saw her use every obstacle as a stepping stone while operating in wisdom not to make the same mistakes over and over. Do you think she prayed for a husband? She will tell you "heck no." She was building a relationship with God when her husband approached her. She pushed him away many times, but God kept guiding her!

I asked her, "Tell me what healing means to you."

Well to be honest I was angry with myself and angry with God. I had called myself doing things the right way and it just seemed to lead to failure. I was like, God, it wasn't supposed to end up this way, I did everything right. But the true question was had I?

Eventually, I had to answer that question and be honest with myself and that's how I moved on. I mean it takes two to make a marriage work. Had I done everything that I should have, had I said some things I shouldn't have said, did I pray enough, did I really trust God in the midst of all that was going on? Even though he didn't do things to make the situation easier or better, what was my role? When we stand before God on judgment day, he won't ask us about all the things that people did and what they did to us. His only concern will be what did you do and how did you respond?

Ultimately, I had to forgive him for his part and I had to forgive myself for my part. When I did that, God didn't push me aside but he blessed me even more!!!

While going through the healing process you must rely heavily upon God to reveal to you the things that are holding you back and ask him to lead you and guide you through the process. Go through the process with your heart and soul holding nothing back. Live the abundant life that has been given to you. Scriptures to reflect upon are:

- *He sends forth his word and heals them and rescues them from the pit and destruction. Psalms 107:20.*
- *Then shall your light break forth like the morning, and your healing shall spring forth speedily, your righteousness shall go before you, and the glory of the Lord shall be your rear guard. Isaiah 58:8.*

Reflection

To thrive, self-reflection is needed. This is where you learn about yourself. You take this time to learn your beliefs, values; why do you have these beliefs and values and where did they come from? What are your goals, behavior, and state of mind? Are you a negative person or positive person? Do you see the glass half empty or half full? Are you proactive or reactive? Are you an introverted person or extroverted person? What are your strengths and weaknesses, and how can you make your weaknesses stronger? Are you performing at your peak capacity and if not, what can you do differently? Self-reflection is needed as often as possible. Self-reflection will help you solve inner conflicts within yourself to receive clarity.

Knowing your strengths and weaknesses helps you recognize and pinpoint areas where you can perform at your peak and areas where you need to strengthen and develop. For example, my strengths are in writing. I have always been the type of person who can sit down and write a 10 page paper in one night and get an A, but my presentation skills are my weakness. I have always been a little shy and timid, so I hide behind paper. I express myself in writing better; therefore, I have always operated at my peak in this area.

My husband is the total opposite. He is an extroverted person. When he walks into the room, he demands the room. He was a car salesperson for 12 years so his presentation skills are on point. He could sell ice to an Eskimo in Alaska, but his writing skills are his weakness. Before he sends anything out by email, he always wants me to proof it.

The important factor is that we need to identify our strengths and weaknesses and know what areas we can focus on for growth and development. We must step out of comfort zone. In order to do that, we have to see ourselves where we are and where we need to be.

My favorite scriptures on self-reflection are:

- *Keep a close watch on yourself and on the teaching. Persist in this, for by doing so you will save both yourself and your hearers. (NIV: 1 Timothy 4:16)*
- *For if anyone thinks he is something and he is nothing, he deceives himself. (NIV: Galatians 6:3)*

Imagination

"Creativity is the process of bringing something new into being. Creativity requires passion and commitment. It brings to our awareness what was previously hidden and points to new life." ~ Unknown

To thrive, your imagination is needed. To use your imagination you need to be creative to think of alternate solutions. If the process you are using now is not working, now is the time to explore and be creative. I know you have heard the definition of insanity is to do the same thing over again and expect different results. Now is the time to try something different. Ask God to lead you and guide you to give you direction on things to change and the process to take. God will guide you by giving you divine ideas.

For example, one way I used my imagination to be creative in the workplace was when I saw a process that was broken. It involved too many middle man people and I often thought, "Why don't they just do it this way?" After researching and visualizing a better process, I prepared a written narrative and visual diagram explaining this process and submitted it to my boss. She reviewed the process and viewed it as a valuable solution to a broken process and submitted it to her boss. This became the new process and is still in operation to this day. It was then that she began to see the value in me. I followed the proper steps and went up the chain of command while earning her trust and respect in the process.

Vision

"Where there is no vision, the people perish: but he that keepeth the law, happy is he."
(NIV: Proverbs 29:18)

Vision is so important to THRIVE! Without vision, people perish. You must know the clear vision for yourself. Vision involves seeing things into existence. Don't look at where you are now, that is in the reflection phase. See where you want to be, what God has showed you…write those things down and visualize it, verbalize it, and memorize it. Think of these areas when you are writing your vision:

- What position do you want to have
- What salary do you want to receive
- What job duties do you want your job to entail
- How many people do you want to employ or supervise
- In what capacity do you want to use your gifts for ministry

I have read there are three kinds of people in the world:

1. People who are never aware of what is happening around them.
2. People who ask, "What just happened?"
3. People who MAKE things happen.

Which one are you? Myles Munroe explains in his book "The Principles and Power of Vision" that vision is your primary motivator. Without it, your life will have no sense of direction, no meaning, no value.

After you have established your vision, write the plan of action to get you there. For example, this is what I have written down:

My Purpose:	To live my life free to **serve God's people**. To be a loving mother and supportive wife. To be an inspiration to women. To encourage

	and motivate women to walk in their purpose.
My Mission Statement:	To be free in every area of my life using my God given abilities in **administration** to **serve others**.
My Vision:	To be in an **administration** position to **serve others** while utilizing my project management experience to be instrumental to the growth of the company. In addition, I want to have my own business to assist others reach their full potential in the areas of administration, earning a total income of $300,000 or more to finance the Kingdom and assist others that are going through the process while serving. I will do this by walking in my purpose, operating in my passion, and seeking God for direction.

That's my vision. In addition to that, I wrote down goals I want to accomplish in 30 days, 90 days, 1 year, 3 years, and 5 years. Some goals I have reached and other goals are still in the process. This book is one of my three year goals in addition to doing seminars and conferences.

What key words do you see in my vision, mission statement, and purpose? SERVE, MOTIVATE, ENCOURAGE, ADMINISTRATION. Your purpose, mission, and vision should include serving in some capacity. We are put here on this earth to serve.

Eliminate and Engage

As we stated in Chapter 1, to thrive you must go through the process of elimination and engage with people who will encourage you and strengthen you. It is during this time that you see what things and people are beneficial to you and what things are toxic to you. You need people in your corner to support, encourage, and mentor you. Everyone who wants to thrive must have a support partner or support group. I have always been told, "If you are the smartest person in your circle then you are in the wrong circle."

The people you engage with are instrumental to your development and instrumental to how your future will become. You will be strongly influenced by the people who you surround yourself with. Your social group will define you in the following ways:

- Your values – what you find important and what really matters
- Your interests – what will occupy your time
- Your personality – how you talk and how you treat others

It is important that you are clear with your social group about your vision, goals, and aspirations, and you will find you will engage with certain people that have likeminded aspirations as you do. For example, one person in the group may come to you if they are desiring to start a business, but then they may go to another person in the group if they want to complain about their job.

I had to go through the process of elimination to the point that it I had to move to another city to change my surroundings. In Illinois, I went to the club every weekend using my bill $ to buy alcohol and outfits to wear out every weekend. I was looking for love in all the wrong places to fill the void in my life. I had no respect for myself and little respect for others. I was on welfare, a single mother, hopeless, deprived, and broke.

I wanted change and I knew the only way to change as fast as I wanted was to start over. I packed my bags and my daughter and I moved to Memphis, TN. I got involved in a loving church and served. I was not interested in dating; my only goal was to build a relationship with God. I spent nights stretched out on the floor praying and surrendering to God. My daughter and I prayed every night and she would pray for brothers and sisters.

I met my husband on the alter during noon day prayer. God revealed to both of us at the same time that we would be married. Seven months later, we were married. My daughter got her prayers answered. My husband had two girls (twins) so she instantly got her prayer of sisters, and then on my wedding night our first daughter was conceived. Now, we have a total of six children, 5 girls and1 boy.

I started off working in the hospital for $10/hour and worked myself up from there. I went back to school to get my MBA and haven't looked back. God has blessed me beyond measure, but I had to go through the process of elimination. I tell others, "If you want to stay in my past, you are not entitled to my future."

I encourage you take on this mindset. If they are not for the "new you" they don't have the privilege of engaging with "the new you" because the "old you" no longer exists.

I have provided some basic tools and steps to take as you enter the process to THRIVE.

Thriving Tools:
1. Be ready to overcome adversity. You have to be tenacious in this process. Every successful person who has worked their way into success had to go through adversity and they got through it and so can you.
2. Healing is needed to prosper and flourish. Now is the time to let go of any unforgiveness, bitterness, or resentment you may have been holding onto. It is your time to THRIVE and live the abundant life that has been given to you.
3. Self-reflection is needed to know where you are so you can take the proper steps to get to where you want to go. Spend at little time daily reflecting over your day's experiences and how you handled things and how they could've been handled differently. I suggest writing your notes down so you can reflect over them and see the progress you are making.
4. Imagination is needed to bring the creative side out. Begin to think of ways that you can change things that are not working in your career, family, finances, and health. Write it down, research other ways, and think of a possible solution.
5. Begin to think of your vision. Where do you see your career or business going? Write it down. Visualize it and verbalize it. Make a plan of action to include 30 days, 90 days, 1 year, 3 years, and 5 years.
6. Go through the process of elimination. Find out who is for you and who is not. Eliminate to Elevate. Find out what is toxic for you and replace that with something that is beneficial to you. For example, if you watch too many reality shows, replace that with inspirational shows on TBN or listen to audio tapes or read inspirational books.

Thriving Points to Consider:

How have you overcome adversity in the past and how will you do it different moving forward?

What do you need healing of and what are the steps you will take to go through the healing process?

Are you a reactive person or proactive person?

Examples of how you have been proactive or reactive (whatever you listed above)?

Are you a negative person or positive person (ask someone close to you if you are not sure)?

What values and beliefs do you hold dear to you and where did you get them from?

Are you a trustworthy person (ask someone close to you if you are not sure)?

Processes you see not working:	*Possible process/solution to turn this problem around:*
Family/Relationships:	

Finances:	
Career/Job/Business/Organization:	
Health/Fitness:	
Other:	

What is your purpose?	
What is your mission statement?	

What is your vision?	
30 day Goal:	
Plan of Action to reach 30 day goal?	
60 day Goal: **Plan of action to reach 60 day goal?**	

What keywords do you see in your purpose, mission statement, and vision?

Thriving Additional Resources:

- Book – *The Principles and Power of Vision* by Dr. Myles Munroe

Thriving Prayer:

Disclaimer: This prayer involves a vow. If you are not willing to hold up to the vow don't say it.

God, I thank you for the opportunity to go through this process to THRIVE. I need you to guide me and direct me. Help to me see people who are for me and things that are toxic to me and give me the strength to go through the process of elimination. I pray that you help me to be creative using my imagination for process of improvement. As I self-reflect, show me who I am and what I need to do to be more like you. Give me the strength and temperament to overcome adversity and use all adversity as a process to grow. God I know your Word says you wish above all that I prosper and be in good health and I stand on that Word knowing I can do all things through Christ that strengthens in you. Help me as I write my vision and make it plain so that those who see it may run with it. I decree and declare favor, blessings, and increase over my life and my vow to you is as I thrive I will continue to serve and empower others in the process. In Jesus' Name. AMEN!

Thriving Confession:

I am prosperous in every area of my life. My vision will come to pass and flourish and help others. I am operating in favor, blessings, and increase and super natural doors are open to me that no man can take the credit for. I am a financer of the kingdom and willing servant of the kingdom, therefore I shall reap the rewards and benefits because will God will give me the desires of my heart as I seek the Kingdom first. I am operating to my full potential daily using my time wisely only to those things that are beneficial to me. I declare this in Jesus name. Amen!

The Wheel Has Come Full Circle

What goes up must come down.
No colors can define who you are.
You may own a cart or limousine.
We'll still reach the end when it is near.
I may be poor today and eat from trash.
Tomorrow, you can't tell. I'll earn some cash.
The bed where you lie is soft and wide.
I sleep at a sidewalk and the stars are my lamp.
You wake up each morn' with a feast on your table
While we are scavenging to fill stomachs when we're able.
Our destiny isn't written in the stars.
We work for a living to thrive in this life.
Be thankful every morning you witness the sun
And pray tonight that no one lives same as I.
Wheels come in full circle, rolling round and round.
Today you'll be on top,
I am watching from the ground.
Let us bear in our minds that we are better than birds.
Our loving Father ensures each mouth is fed.
Not even the smallest details can pass by His eyes.
So plant a seed of kindness and reap a better life.

~Unknown

CHAPTER 4
STARTING POINT

As you become more clearer about who you really are, you'll be better able to understand what is best for you.~ Oprah Winfrey

Mistakes are painful when they happen, but years later a collection of mistakes are called experiences. ~ Unknown

Now that we have talked about the shifting your paradigm and the principles of THRIVE, let's start the process.

No Limits, No Excuses

You can be born into a nightmare, but God can usher you into living the dream!~ Tyler Perry

What is holding you back from reaching your destiny and fulfilling your purpose? What have you been through that someone else has not been through and has overcome? Were you molested? Read Tyler Perry and Oprah Winfrey's testimony...they also were molested. Were you homeless? Again, read Tyler Perry's testimony. Were you in an abusive relationship (physical or verbal)? I was physically and verbally abused. Did you have to file bankruptcy and start all over? So did Bill Gates. Are you on welfare and can't see a way around it? I've been there. There is nothing you can tell me you have or are currently going through to justify you staying in the same position you are in now.

When you have excuses, ask yourself, "Where are these excuses coming from?" Is it fear? A lot of excuses come from fear. Kick all of your fears, excuses, limits and barriers to the curb. Quit living in a box. You will be buried in a box so live your life to the fullest.

I had to get rid of fear and excuses. The fact that you are reading this book now has proven that I had to get rid of fear and excuses. For years, I've told myself, "Nobody will read my book. My story is no different from anyone else's story. I'm not successful enough yet." Then, God told me, "You have a story to tell and your purpose is to inspire others….so tell your story." Successful people don't quit. They are not shackled by fear and doubt. They sacrifice. They live outside the box. Small victories and accomplishments motivate the successful person and they use that same motivation to motivate someone else. Les Brown said, "There is no safe place in life."

My daughter had a terrible accident when she was two years old. She fell through the banister about 10 feet and hit her head on the hardwood floor. She had bleeding on the brain and in the brain. The doctors said she would probably be mentally retarded and slow. I let fear kick in when she was four years old and wasn't talking, but I didn't give up. I began to take her to speech therapy three times a week. She began to talk.

When she started school, they wanted to diagnosis her with ADHD, hold her back, and make her take Special Ed classes. I said "No….she will not be diagnosed with ADHD and she will not be held back…we will get her grades up." I found a tutor who worked with her three days a week and I began to work with her nightly. Now, to God be the glory, she is a 14 year old who makes Honor Roll, loves to read like her mom, and gets paid to tutor other children in after school. She has not been diagnosed with ADHD, she is on no medication, she was not held back, and now she talks too much!

Naturally, everyone has doubts and experiences fear before embarking on any goal. Just know, you have to try! Put your seed in the ground. Water it. Watch it grow. Watch it blossom. Then comes the harvest! The best remedy of fear is activity. Get active! THRIVE!

Be Content Where You Are

It is important to be content where you are, but it is still necessary to strive for better. You can be joyous where you are and still set goals to achieve more. In the previous chapter, we discussed when we go through the self-reflection stage, that is where we discover what brings us joy. Operating in your purpose is one thing that will bring you joy in addition to other factors. When you have joy on the inside, it will carry over to the outside regardless of your circumstances. Just because you are content does not mean you have to remain stagnant. Your joy does not depend on external factors such as wealth, promotions, luxury cars or houses. Happiness is based on outer circumstances, joy is from within. Happiness is state of circumstance whereas joy is a state of being.

In the book "Why We Do What We Do: Understanding Self-motivation" by Edward Deci, the author explains two different aspirations:

1. Intrinsic – people who are satisfied with having good relationships, contributing to your community, and growing as an individual.
2. Extrinsic – people who associate success with being wealthy, famous, and good looking.

Author Deci conveys in his book the problem with the extrinsic person is they rely heavily on outward elements and depend on others. The problem with this is when/if the outer wealth and good looking disappears, so does their self-worth. Often times, even when the aspirations of wealth and fame are obtained, the extrinsic people still are not happy.

There is a difference between striving for excellence and perfection. Excellence is internal, involving setting a high standard for yourself. Perfection is external, setting standards based upon someone's expectations. You will never be happy when you set your standards based upon someone's expectations of you. I always strive for excellence by doing the best I can do, and if that is not up to standard on someone's level, then at least I know I gave it my all! If you aim for excellence, success is sure to follow!

Always Strive for Better

Remember, it's not all about you. If you think you have enough and you don't need more, continue to strive to help others who need a helping hand or assist others who are going through what you came out of.

By Striving to do the impossible men have always reached at least the possible ~ Unknown

God put you here on earth for a reason and I guarantee it was not for you to live comfortably and just look out for yourself. Always strive for better. Don't stay in survival mode. Don't live a life hopeless, without meaning, without vision. Don't ever discredit the experiences you gained along the way. They have made you stronger, wiser, and now you have a story to tell to inspire others. Use your trials as a lesson to prepare you for your destiny. Once you have reached one of your goals, set another one. Once you are walking in your purpose, extend it to reach more people.

The two most important days in our life is when we are born and when we realize why we were born –
Pastor Marron Thomas.

When I say strive for better, I am not just talking about monetary or fame. I'm talking about strive for better by walking in your purpose and helping others to do the same. Strive for better by operating in your passion and love the work you are doing. Strive for better by what you are doing now and get paid $8.00/hour to do it… start your own business doing the same thing and get paid twice as much while offering employment to others. Strive for better by experiencing joy on the inside and letting it flow outward. Strive for better in how you approach life and the lens from which you look at things by not being reactive, but proactive.

My agreement partner and who I consider a friend Patricia McNair, is a great visionary with a big heart to help people. She is successful, but she does not use her success as an excuse to live comfortably. She continues to expand her arms to reach out to others in the community in the area God has called her – education. 5 for 5 is a non-profit organization that relates education and home ownership. She saw a problem, but instead of focusing on the problem, God gave her the solution. She made a commitment to be PROACTIVE by contributing to saving the lives of our youth rather than REACTIVE. One of my pet peeves is hearing people constantly focusing on the problem. For example, complaining about the youth but not supporting any organizations or businesses that are trying to reach out to help our youth.

It is important to always strive for better for yourself and your family. However, it is more important to strive for better by helping and serving others.

So How Do You Start Where You Are and Begin to Thrive?

When I think of thriving where you are, I am reminded of my favorite movie, "Facing the Giants." The coach was going through a difficult time in his life. He was considered a failure, his job was in jeopardy, his car was on its last leg, and he was struggling financially. Then he had a revelation from God. He began to operate in his purpose and thrive and at that point his whole situation turned around. He began to win in more ways than one. He had a debt free, brand new car sowed to him, he got a raise, his wife became pregnant, and he won the championship. Where did he start?

He did an analysis of where he was in the beginning of the movie. He looked at where he wanted to go and where God wanted to lead him. He started with seeking God and finding his purpose. When he found his purpose, his mentality changed from working as a coach to a football team to serving God's people. He was **tenacious**. He was faced with adversity, but his vision brought him through it.

He went through the **healing** process. He was upset and hurt because he felt like people had betrayed him and was hurt because he was told he couldn't give his wife children. However, he told God, "I will still love you regardless." He went through the **reflection** process. He saw where he was, where he team was, and where they needed/wanted to be. He used his **imagination** to be creative by building team strategies relevant to the Bible such as the stone wall and blindfolding his team members to see how much drive was really in them. He wrote a **vision** and made it plain. He also was prepared to do the process of **elimination** by telling his assistant coach if he wasn't for him to leave and he began to **engage** with others who were for him. He also reached out to others to help them by encouraging them with God's word. He went through the THRIVE process and reaped the benefits of overflow.

Thriving Tools:

1. First be content where you are. Have joy on the inside and let it flow outward.
2. Always strive for better. Don't become stagnant. Strive for better for yourself and strive for better by helping others.
3. Do an analysis of where you are now. What is your current situation? Are you working in a job that you don't like? Are you living paycheck to paycheck? Do you feel hopeless and empty?
4. Find your purpose. What are you here on earth for? What is your passion? What are your gifts? After you discover the answer to these questions, operate in your purpose. If you can't incorporate your passion and gifts in your current workplace or business, volunteer somewhere to do it. You will find a sense of completion, security, and fulfillment when you are operating in your purpose rather than feeling empty, hopeless and barely surviving. I recommend reading Rick Warren's "The Purpose Driven Life: What on Earth Am I Here For" to assist you in this area.
5. If you are employed, change your mentality from working to serving. When you have a mentality of serving, you have a better attitude of doing your job. My favorite quote is "The Best Way to Serve God is to Serve Other People" ~ Rick Warren. When you change your mindset to serving, your whole demeanor changes. Don't look at your current job as working for the "white man." Look at your current position as serving God's people just as God served his people and do it with a mentality of Christ. God loved to serve his people. He washed their feet, served them food, and served in a

variety of ways. If your employer asks you to clean the toilet, clean as though God himself was going to walk through the bathroom and reward you for a job well done.

Thriving Points to Consider:

Where are you now? What don't you like about where you are now and why?

What are some areas you want to change?

What are your strengths? What is your passion (gifts)?

What can you do NOW to begin to operate your strengths and gifts?

How can you change your mentality from working to serving?

What are the struggles and experiences that are holding you back?

Research and read the testimony or a story of someone who you admire that has gone through some of the same struggles you listed above, overcame them and is walking in their destiny. How did they get through it? What steps did they take?

What are ways you can be TENACIOUS in your current situation(s)?

What are some HEALING steps you can apply?

What are some ways you can use your IMAGINATION to be creative in your current situation?

Thriving Additional Resources:

- Movie – *Facing the Giants*
- Book – Rick Warren – *The Purpose Driven Life*
- Book – Edward Deci - *Why We Do What We Do*

Thriving Prayer:

God, I thank you for where I am today and for the joy that I have within and is flowing out. I thank you for giving me the strength to always strive for better in my personal life and by helping others. I thank you for the mindset of No Limits, No Excuses. I thank you for opening my eyes to see what has been holding me back. God show me areas I need to change and help me in those areas. Help me to put on the mindset of serving while reaping the benefits. Your Word says if I seek the Kingdom first, all other things will be added. Lord, I thank you for every struggle and obstacle that I have endured and I thank you for your grace and mercy. God I pray that I am operating in excellence and not perfection, but always putting my all into my work. I want my work to be pleasing to you. In Jesus' Name.

Thriving Confession:

I am content and happy with my life now and I am striving for better. Nothing will stop me as I strive for better. Nothing will hold me back as I continue to press forward to operate in my passion and gifts and inspire others. I will be proactive rather than reactive. I will focus on solutions rather than problems. I will not complain about problems, but I will seek ways to help solve problems. I serve God's people with an attitude of Love. I love to serve. I live to serve. I will seek God's Kingdom first knowing all things will be added. I know God will give me the desires of my heart if I obey Him for his Word says obedience is better than sacrifice. I know I will thrive in areas of my life. In Jesus' Name.

The Mind Is the Battle Ground

The mind starts every battle.
Dreams are pictures that are in your mind;
You can sleep, but your mind is always awake.
Everything that goes to heart starts in the mind,
Even things that goes to mouth starts in the mind.
Your deeds are controlled by the mind.
For the mind is the battle ground.

The mind captures a thousand pictures in a second,
It stores everything you see.
Hearing feeds the mind with information,
Information creates pictures.
If you realize how powerful your thoughts are,
You would never think negative.

For the mind is the battlefield!

An idle mind is the devil's workshop;
Failure starts in the mind.
In the province of the mind,
What you believe is true or becomes true.
Let your brain be your servant instead of your master;
Rule it instead of allowing it to rule you.
For the mind is the battle ground!
Bad thoughts can be deleted;
The mind can be restored.
Your mindset can change.
For imagination is greater than knowledge.
The mind is the battlefield.

Your blessings are near,
But your mind is far.
You cannot have access to your blessings,
Until you change your mindset.
True enjoyment comes from the activity of the mind,
And exercise of the body;
the two are ever united.
For the mind dominates the body.

When the devil steals your mind,
He kills your soul;
Thus you are destroyed.
Be transformed by the renewing of your mind.
Keep God in your mind,
And you shall be kept in perfect peace.
For the mind is the battle ground.

~ **Lucky Zwane**

CHAPTER 5

POSITION YOURSELF

You are not only responsible for your life, but doing the best at this moment puts you in the best place for the next moment. ~Oprah Winfrey

Get Your Mind Right

If you get your mind going in the right direction your life will begin to go in the right direction ~ Unknown.

For as a man thinks in his heart, so is he ~ (NIV: Proverbs 23:7)

Thriving is more than a state of mind. It does require action, but first it must start in your mind. Another one of my favorite sayings is "Where the mind goes, the man follows." Success and failure begins with a thought. Our thoughts affect every area of life – relationships, finances, self-image, health, work and business.

No one has more power over you than yourself other than God and that is a good thing because God wants you to be successful. The only thing separating you from the successful people whom you admire is your state of mind. They had it made it up in their mind failure is not an option. Even if you don't succeed the first time…. you are not a failure because remember as we discussed in Chapter 1, we take all lessons learned as stepping stones to thrive. So again, FAILURE IS NOT AN OPTION. Because the first time didn't turn out as planned, that is a stepping stone because you have learned what to do differently the next time.

Use your stumbling blocks as stepping stones. building blocks.

I have come to admire this attitude in my husband. At first, I didn't understand it, but now that my mindset has changed, I admire and love him for his drive and determination. My husband is a great visionary. He sees things already complete and successful. I'm an administrative person so while he's calculating the millions at the end I'm calculating the thousands to get it started.

Regardless of my voice or any other voice, that didn't stop his drive. If it didn't work the first time, he would come with something bigger the next week. He said failure is not an option. This is coming from a high school dropout raised in the projects with 13 brothers and sisters from a single parent home. Because of his mindset of FAILURE IS NOT AN OPTION he is an author, entrepreneur, and a community activist known as the Mayor of Frayser. He is well respected and admired by many. Success is a choice, but first it must start in your mind. You must visualize it and vocalize it.

When I think of visualizing you are successful, you visualize it so much you call it into existence, I think about the law of attraction and the movie that has made a lasting impact of my life called "The Secret." This movie gives sound principles about how to change your mind to THRIVE to where you actually attract it. Positive thinking can change your life beyond measures.

I also love the book "Battlefield of the Mind" by Joyce Meyers. In this book, the author provides steps to help train your mind every day with uplifting thoughts toward yourself and others. She explains how the mind is the battlefield – it is where you win or lose. You must renew your mind on a daily basis. This is ongoing. The battle in your mind will continue as long as you are on this earth. Those negative thoughts of failure, hopelessness, loss, and devastation will come, but you must renew your mind with thoughts of love, power, grace, and victory. You do whatever it takes. Sometimes you may have to look at yourself in the mirror and say "I am the VICTOR and not the VICTIM, GREATER IS HE THAT IS IN ME THAN HE THAT IS IN THE WORLD, I AM BEAUTIFULLY AND WONDERFULLY MADE, I AM AN OVERCOMER, I CAN DO ALL THINGS THROUGH CHRIST THAT STRENGTHENS IN ME."

You do whatever you have to do to turn those negative thoughts into positive thoughts. I have downloaded the "Battlefield of the Mind" devotion on You Version and I start my day off reading this. Throughout the day, if a negative thought tries to pop into my mind, I go into the bathroom and read that devotion over and over again and meditate on that throughout the day. Remember, when someone accepts Christ as Lord and Savior, they receive a new spirit and new heart from God, but not a new mind because this must be renewed requiring it to be transformed by the renewal of mind and attitude (NIV: Romans 12:2).

The Bible presents a lot of detailed instructions on what kind of thoughts we should think. Philippians 4:8 tells us to think of things that build us up and not tear us down. The more time we spend thinking on these things, the more power we have over our mind. Once we have power over our mind, we have the power to change our situation.

How To Train Your Mind Into Thinking Positive

You can train your mind into thinking positive by replacing negative thoughts with positive thoughts.

| I am broke. | I thank God for giving me wisdom to utilize my finances more efficiently so I can THRIVE. |

I will never get off welfare.	I thank God for giving me the opportunity to utilize the system while I am taking the necessary steps to better position myself.
I was molested and now I have all this anger built up inside of me.	I was violated at a young age, but I will forgive the person who violated me because if not, he/she continues to win. I will not let them win any longer. I am not a victim…I am victorious!
I've had to file bankruptcy … twice.	I have not managed my finances well, but I have been given a new start and I will take advantage of this new start. I will manage my finances better and use those trials as stepping stones.
My marriage is over.	I am experiencing problems in my marriage, but I will not give up. All marriages go through tests and this is just a test for our testimony.

For every negative thought,
replace it with a positive thought!

Reposition your mindset and thrive.

Make Sure Your Image Is On Point

A strong positive self-image is the best possible preparation for success ~ Unknown

Personal image is so much more than outward appearance. When someone says your name what image comes to mind? In every position I have been in, I have left a lasting impression. When they say Teresa Landrum, I am known for always smiling. In fact, I have had several people ask me, "Why are you always smiling?" My reply is, "Man didn't give me this smile so man can't take away this smile." I am also known for my personable attitude. To me, no person is higher than the next one. Therefore, I will greet the maid as I would the CEO. Of course, I respect authority so if that person has a salutation I will call or greet that person accordingly. Just because someone is cleaning the floors does not mean they are not worthy of being greeted in a respectful way.

What impression are you making? Are you known for always going over and beyond your job duties to serve others or are you known for always complaining about having more work to do? Your image speaks volumes. In many ways, it will follow you and it may help you thrive or it may hinder you from thriving. What is your self-image? Often times how you see yourself is how others will see you.

If you dress in a way that questions your respect for yourself, be prepared to get treated that way. I've always been told to dress how the person who is in the position you want to obtain dresses. If your finances do not allow you to do that, dress proudly with what you already have to command respect from others just as you give them the respect they deserve.

Get Your Hands On As Much As You Can

While positioning yourself to thrive, it is time for you to extend outside your horizons. Don't be afraid to start new things. Getting involved as much as your time allows to position you to network with a variety of people and also gets you cross-trained into doing multiple things. Become an expert in that field by educating yourself and doing research. Know your competition, the mission, goals and objectives of that business or organization. If you are an employee, prove to your boss that you are willing to do more and always offer a hand to everyone. No job is too small. If you see someone walking in struggling carrying a big load of boxes, offer help. If you see housekeeping struggling to throw away the trash, offer help. Remember again, as discussed previously, you are serving God and God does not discriminate on who you serve. No one is too high or too low. In God's eyes, everyone is equal. When you offer your assistance, do it with a cheerful heart.

If you are an entrepreneur, get involved in as many network and marketing events as possible. Attend as many events as possible. As my husband would say, become a 3V Leader – one who is visible, vocal, and valuable.

Work Hard, But More Importantly, Work Smart

Working hard is very important, but working smarter is more important. You're not going to get anywhere without working extremely hard, but that does not mean overextend your boundaries. It is important to know your boundaries otherwise you will get burnt out in the process.

For me, I know it is important for me to always take a lunch. I always have to leave the building even if it means going into my car and listening to music or reading a book. I know this is my boundary. By me knowing my boundaries, I am able to go out for lunch, come back and continue to serve with a cheerful spirit. I am able to greet everyone I encounter with a genuine smile.

Also with setting boundaries, learn how to keep your personal business separate from work. Don't carry your personal baggage into the workplace. Don't let your personal troubles affect your smile. When you walk through the doors, leave your personal problems at the door. Do not let it affect you serving God's people. People in the hospital have a saying, "Do what's best for the patient." People at restaurants say, "Do what's best for the customers." I say, "Serve God's people like he did" and that will encompass everyone and everything you do. If you keep the mentality of serving God's people, there is no way you can go wrong.

The movie "Pursuit of Happyness" comes to mind when I think of Positioning Yourself to Thrive. Based on a true story, Will Smith, who plays Chris Gardner, was going through some difficult times in his life. He was having financial problems, business wasn't doing well, his wife left him, his car was down, he was homeless and single father. BUT, he had the mindset of *Failure wasn't an option*. His outward appearance wasn't on point, but his self-image was. He told his wife, "I got this, it will work out." He began to position himself by doing an internship while doing his business on the side. He didn't give up. He worked smart – he calculated how many calls he could make in an hour by not drinking a lot of water, therefore not having to take as many bathroom breaks. He studied after he put his son down for the night. As a result, it paid off in the end. He was selected out of a class of 50 to join the company full time.

Thriving Tools:

1. Get your mind right. Make up your mind that failure is not an option. Visualize receiving your promotion and verbalize your goals as much as possible. Visualize your business growing with a profit of six figures employing 30 people. Verbalize "My business is successful and prospering every day."

2. Get your self-image right. Look at yourself in the mirror and see how beautiful you are and say "God made me in his

image therefore I am beautiful." Also, make sure your outward appearance is on point. If you only have one pair of pants – make sure those are clean and creased and walk into that office or business as if they were tailor made.

3. Get your hands on as much as you can. Expand your horizons. Offer help as much as possible. When you have extra time, do your research. Find out who your competition is, what is the mission, history, and goals of the business or organization.

Thriving Positioning Points to Consider:

Name some areas in your life where you have been successful.

Name some areas in your life where things didn't go as planned and list what you can do differently.

What lasting impression have you left in your previous jobs or business?

What lasting impression do you want to leave moving forward?

What are some additional duties you can take on in your current job or business to expand your horizons?

Thriving Additional Resources:

- Book – Charlie Caswell - *How to Become Visible, Vocal, and Valuable to your Community*
- Book – Joyce Meyer – *Battlefield of the Mind*
- Movie – *The Pursuit of Happyness*

Thriving Prayer:

God, I thank you that I am taking on the mindset of Christ. That I am replacing every negative thought with a positive thought and the devil does not have control over my mind. I DO! I thank you that my image is on point and I am leaving a positive impression with everyone I encounter. I thank you that I am working hard and smart and I am proving myself to be a person who is worthy of promotion. I know that as I see the value in myself, others will see the value in me as well. In Jesus' Name.

Thriving Confession:

I have the mindset of Christ. I renew my mind daily with positive thoughts and I operate in that focus all day. My image is on point reflecting I have respect for myself and demanding respect from others. I leave a positive impression with everyone I encounter as a hard worker operating in character and integrity. I will be offered different opportunities, promotions, increase as I walk in favor. Supernatural doors are open for me and I will reap the benefits. I am thriving in every area of my life.
In Jesus' Name!

Phenomenal Woman

Pretty women wonder where my secret lies.
I'm not cute or built to suit a fashion model's size
But when I start to tell them,
They think I'm telling lies.
I say,
It's in the reach of my arms
The span of my hips,
The stride of my step,
The curl of my lips.
I'm a woman
Phenomenally. Phenomenal woman,
That's me.

I walk into a room
Just as cool as you please,
And to a man,
The fellows stand or
Fall down on their knees.
Then they swarm around me,
A hive of honey bees.
I say,
It's the fire in my eyes,
And the flash of my teeth,
The swing in my waist,
And the joy in my feet.
I'm a woman
Phenomenally,
Phenomenal woman,
That's me.

*Men themselves have wondered
What they see in me.
They try so much
But they can't touch
My inner mystery.
When I try to show them
They say they still can't see.
I say,
It's in the arch of my back,
The sun of my smile,
The ride of my breasts,
The grace of my style.
I'm a woman
Phenomenally.
Phenomenal woman,
That's me.*

*Now you understand
Just why my head's not bowed.
I don't shout or jump about
Or have to talk real loud.
When you see me passing
It ought to make you proud.
I say,
It's in the click of my heels,
The bend of my hair,
The palm of my hand,
The need of my care,*

*'Cause I'm a woman
Phenomenally.
Phenomenal woman,
That's me.*

~ **Maya Angelou**

CHAPTER 6
ATTRIBUTES TO HAVE WHILE THRIVING

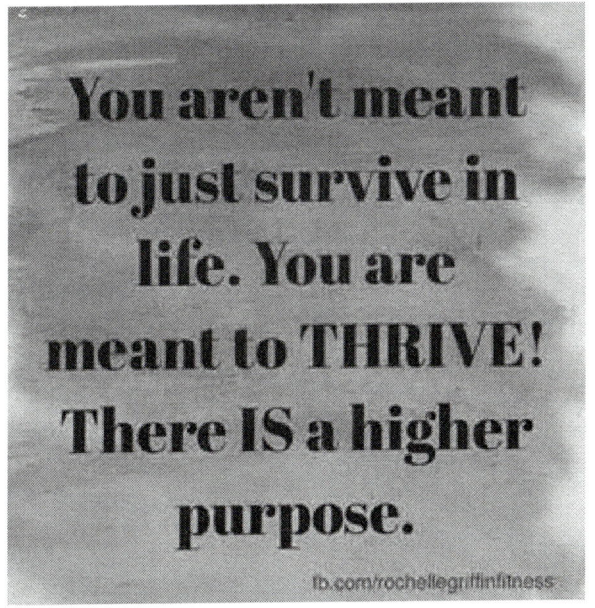

Now that you are positioning yourself to thrive and you have or are working in the areas you need to change, it is important to have certain attributes in the workplace or your business.

As we stated before, professional image is an important factor while thriving. Often times, the first time a person meets you, that image of you will stick with them for a long time until you can prove them otherwise. Again, if you take on the mindset of serving, following the example of Jesus...you will want to represent Him well!

Office Etiquette

Office etiquette is about conducting yourself respectfully and courteously in the workplace. This is important because you are representing the business or organization. If you represent them well, people will notice, and they will respect you accordingly. Regardless of what other people are doing, you have to stand out. Some basic things to consider are:

- Never display any amount of frustration in front of customers. This should never be done. If you are annoyed or irritated, take a break and catch some air. This will project a bad image of the business to the customers and word of mouth spreads fast.

- There is a time to speak with your co-workers about a disagreement. Make sure you are calmed down and you have had the time to think about the situation. Never act on emotions. When the appropriate time has come to talk with your co-worker, do it in a professional way. Tell your co-worker, "When you get a chance, I would like to discuss something with you." When the time comes, go to a place behind closed doors. Speak in a professional tone with good eye contact. Have examples to give your co-worker and let that person know how you felt. If your co-worker begins to get loud and unprofessional, inform them, we will discuss this later and involve a mediator. At this point, you have proven you are more mature and know how to handle things professionally.

- Wear appropriate office attire. Look at how the people dress that are in the position you are trying to obtain and dress on that level if your finances allow you to. Don't dress like the other people who are on the level you are currently at. Remember you are trying to get to another level. Stay away from clothing or piercings that will distract people and give people a perception that you will have to prove that you are different. For example, if you wear tight clothing, you will be perceived as unprofessional. The same applies with tattoos and piercings. Even though tattoos are gaining acceptance in the workplace, it still looks unprofessional. Many CEO's do not want someone with tattoos showing going to a professional meeting to represent the business or organization.

- While it is important to build relationships with co-workers in the workplace, it is also important to stay out of cliques. You want to show your employer you are able to engage with a diverse group of individuals. If possible, try to go to lunch with different individuals and groups within your workplace. Also, this will help you get information about the business from different perspectives and you will gain some valuable knowledge along the way.

- Always follow through on your assignments and special projects. When given an assignment ask, "When do you need this by?" This will help you to prioritize your assignments to get things done in a timely manner. Always try to turn your assignment in 1-2 days before the deadline date in case there are any changes that need to be made.

- Build your trust with any supervisor and co-workers. With your supervisor, always follow the proper chain of command. Take the problem or request to them first, then if they give you permission, escalate it as needed. Always copy your boss on emails regarding things they may need to be informed of and anything you send to their boss. Build your co-workers trust by following through and keeping your word on things you say you are going to do. If trust has been broken in the past, send an email confirming what was discussed to leave a paper trail.

Don't Expect Praise or Appreciation from Anyone Other Than God

It's only natural to desire and crave appreciation and praise when you feel that you are doing a good job, but just know, it may not always come. It is during those times we feel unappreciated and undervalued, but I've learned "Validation comes from above." All the validation you need is in the Bible. Tell yourself what God says about you and say this prayer:

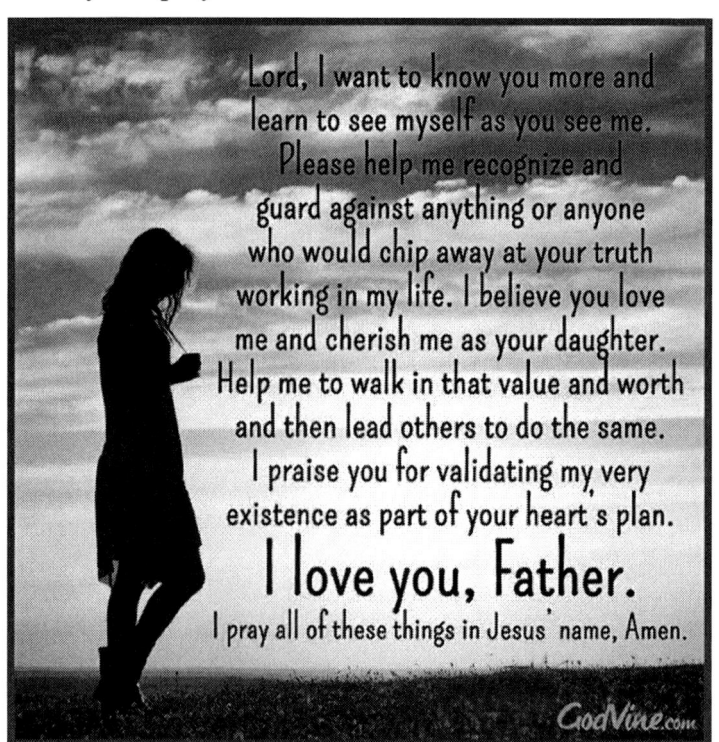

You will notice once you stop seeking validation and confirmation from others, you will attract it. People are drawn to people who know who they are and know their worth, People shouldn't validate your worth. It's nice to receive validation, but don't expect it…don't let it determine your happiness. When you get the opportunity, give validation, praises and confirmation to others.

Lead By Example

John Maxwell has been instrumental in me growing as a leader. There is a difference between a leader and manager. A leader motivates, inspires, and empowers people, whereas a manager manages tasks and people. It is possible you can be both, but a leader is what we are going to talk about now. Telling people what to do does not inspire and motivate people. You have to lead by example. You can be a leader and not a manager. You can make the decision to be a leader now regardless of what position you are in.

If you ask others to show good customer service and respect others, you must do the same. If you expect others to be on time and only take 30 minute lunches, you should do the same. Regardless of what you see other people around you doing, you be the leader and do what you know is best. This is how you stand-out and THRIVE!

Breaking the Glass Ceiling

At some point, you may feel like you have reached the level where you have gone as far as you can go. You can see the next level of promotion, but somehow there seems to be barriers that are stopping you. This is what is called the glass ceiling in the natural, but we know that there is no glass ceiling when you have the mentality of no limits, no excuses. Originally, this term was used to apply to women and minorities, but that is no longer the case. We now have women who are CEO's of Fortune 500 companies and soon to be a woman President (YES, I am speaking it into existence.) It's time to smash that glass and walk through with purpose and determination. It's time to THRIVE! Just know, "Nothing is impossible with God."

It's time to research:

- Research the key competencies of the skill set, education level, and attributes of people in the position you want to obtain.
- Do a thorough research of the company. What are the values, vision, mission, history? Who is their competition? What areas have they expanded in and what areas do they want to expand in?

After you have completed a thorough research of the company, now it is time to be proactive. Let your boss know you are looking to advance within the company. Inform her of the education and skills you have (they may have forgotten) and ask her what areas she feels you need to develop to get into a position like the one you are desiring. Use that input and grow from there.

Set your action plan. Build your network. Engage in professional development opportunities. Update your resume. Get involved with as many cross-functional opportunities as possible to develop and enhance the skill set you need. Begin to expand your network outside of the company. In case you are not able to break the glass ceiling in your current company, you will be preparing yourself to go elsewhere. Know that your promotion may not come right away. It could take months or even years, but you are being proactive and continue to THRIVE where you are.

To THRIVE where you are while attempting to break the glass ceiling, it is important to consider these options:

- Do work that you enjoy utilizing your gifts and passion. As I stated before, I went outside my passion and was miserable despite the fact I got paid more money. It is important to stay in the field you enjoy doing. If you encounter obstacles and barriers in a position where you are operating in your passion, you will still stay motivated and driven. In addition, you will excel in your work and get noticed for your accomplishments.

- Become visible, vocal, and valuable. Raise your professional image by learning to see yourself as an expert in your field. Raise your visibility and showcase your gifts by training others. Start a blog, do a newsletter, write something to show how much knowledge you have in your field. If you are not able to do it in your current position at your company or business, start by promoting on social media and encourage your friends and support system to become engaged.

- Seek out mentors. Begin to seek mentors that are THRIVING in the position you want to achieve. Look to these people to teach you the necessary skills and introduce you to the people you need to know. Watch them. Study them. Research them. Ask them for feedback and direction on how to advance.

- Build up your professional portfolio. Anytime you receive positive feedback, awards, and recognition, put them in a binder to present at the appropriate time. Keep documentation on projects you have completed.

Operate in Character and Integrity

Success will come and go, but integrity is forever. ~ **Unknown**

Until a person can say deeply and honestly, I am what I am today because of the choices I've made yesterday, that person cannot say, I choose otherwise.

~ **Stephen R. Covey**

Character defines you. That is who you are. You can have a reputation for having positive character or negative character. This is a description of your personal attributes, traits, and abilities. A woman who is noble and operates in character is hard to find in the workplace. It seems we have to prove ourselves more and therefore we go through great extremes to do so, but we must not jeopardize our values and beliefs.

Integrity is doing the right thing at all times no matter who is watching or the repercussions that will follow. It may take years to build a reputation of integrity, but in a matter of minutes, you can lose it. In some instances, you may never get the opportunity to get it back. To operate in integrity makes you unique. Not many people do this now, but it will follow you a long way. Do not associate yourself with people who are not trustworthy, who are not operating in integrity. If they are not trustworthy with others, they will not be trustworthy with you.

Joyce Meyer talks about in one of her devotions "developed potential without character does not glorify God." She goes on to talk about how if we become a huge success and continue to be mean and harsh to others, it is not pleasing to God.

No one can take character and integrity away from you. Walking in character and integrity is a choice you have to make. Someone may be able to take your life, but character and integrity, you will die with. People will continue to associate you based upon your character and integrity even when you are dead for years.

Be Patient

We live in a generation where we want the microwave blessings. We want instant gratification now, but tell me which one tastes better? Ribs cooked in the microwave or ribs that have been marinated in sauce overnight, seasoned, and then cooked in the oven? To get the results we desire, we have to wait patiently.

Patience is so important anytime you are attempting to THRIVE. Growth and development take time. It will not happen overnight. The power of patience is a part of the transition process. Timelines are important to keep you on track, but they may need to be adjusted. Don't worry. This is part of the process. Don't mistake patience for laziness. Good things come to those who wait and are active while waiting. While you are waiting, you are learning more about yourself which is important.

Sometimes, God can block our progress in an area until He feels we have grown and developed but know that delay is not denial. He knows what it is best. If He releases the blessing too early, will that help you or hurt you? This is why prayer and meditation are also important while being patient. Listen to God's voice. He will speak to you to tell you what He wants from you, where He wants you to grow, and what He wants you to do. As you operate in character and integrity, remember that as you serve God to the best of your ability, you will receive all the validation you need from Him.

When I think about having patience while waiting, I think of the movie "Fireproof." This movie has been a motivational factor in my marriage. My husband and I were having problems on the verge of divorce when we saw this movie and this movie showed me how to be patient while waiting for a change. In this movie, the husband and wife were having problems. They both wanted out, but the husband turned his life and his marriage over to God. He went through the 40 days of the Love Dare and still saw no change. In fact, the situation got worse when his wife began to interact with another man, but that did not deter him. He continued to seek God, learn about himself, grow, develop, and self-reflect on areas he needed to improve. His wife even filed for divorce but still he stood on God's word. In the end, his marriage was restored and even his relationship with his mom was restored. He received double!

Just know there is timing for everything. God knows the right time and he will release it at that time. Continue to grow, develop, learn about yourself, seek God and wait patiently knowing the end result will be worth the wait!

Thriving Tools:

1. Personal image is an important factor while thriving. Make sure your image is on point and walk as the Godly Thriving Woman you are.

2. Always be respectful and courteous in the workplace. Respect authority and represent the business well.

3. Lead by example. Do what you expect of others. Be a leader and not a follower. Ask God to lead you and as you follow him, others will follow you.

4. Operate in character and integrity. Do what you know is right regardless of who is watching. Know what is done in the dark will eventually appear in the light.

5. Don't expect validation from others. The only validation you need is from God.

Thriving Points to Consider:

What are some ways you can change to make sure your personal image is on point?

What are some things you can change to make sure you are always respectful and courteous of others?

Do you currently lead by example? If not, what are some areas you can change to be sure you are?

Do you operate in character and integrity? If not, what are some things you can change to be sure you are?

What are some things you can do while you are patiently waiting on God?

Thriving Additional Resources:

- Book – *Developing the Leader Within You* by John Maxwell
- Movie - *Fireproof*

Thriving Prayer:

God, I thank you for the opportunity to display a Godly image before your people. Help me to have an image that is pleasing to you. Help me to do unto others as I would want them to do unto me and be respectful and courteous at all times. Help me to respect authority and respect people in leadership positions. Help me to learn from the people I need to learn from and to pray for the people I need to pray for and wisdom to know the difference. Help me to lead by example as you lead me. Holy Spirit help me to always operate in character and integrity and to be patient knowing that you have the best plan in store for me and you will release me at the right time. While I wait, help me to continue to learn, grow, develop in my relationships, work ethics, finances; balancing and prioritizing as needed always putting you first. Help me to continue to serve others with a pleasing heart and to encourage others to do the same. In Jesus' Name. Amen!

Thriving Confession:

Father, I thank you that I am a woman of character and integrity. I am a leader and not a follower. Others follow me because of my leadership while I follow you. I thank you for the people in leadership positions you have placed in my life. I thank you that I am an asset to the business/organization and every person I encounter I leave a lasting impression with them of one who is patient, noble, and loves to serve God's people. I know that the road you are preparing before me is blessed, prosperous, and full of advancement opportunities and growth. In Jesus' name!

One Flaw in Women

Women have strengths that amaze men.
They bear hardships and they carry burdens,
but they hold happiness, love and joy.
They smile when they want to scream

They sing when they want to cry.
They cry when they are happy
and laugh when they are nervous.

They fight for what they believe in.
They stand up to injustice.

They don't take "no" for an answer
when they believe there is a better solution.
They go without so their family can have.
They go to the doctor with a frightened friend.
They love unconditionally.

They cry when their children excel
and cheer when their friends get awards.
They are happy when they hear about
a birth or a wedding.
Their hearts break when a friend dies.
They grieve at the loss of a family member,

Yet they are strong when they
think there is no strength left.
They know that a hug and a kiss
can heal a broken heart.

*Women come in all shapes, sizes and colors.
They'll drive, fly, walk, run or e-mail you
to show how much they care about you.*

*The heart of a woman is what
makes the world keep turning.*

*They bring joy, hope and love.
They have compassion and ideas.
They give moral support to their
family and friends.*

*Women have vital things to say
and everything to give.*

**HOWEVER, IF THERE IS ONE FLAW IN WOMEN,
IT IS THAT THEY FORGET THEIR WORTH.**

~ **Unknown**

CHAPTER 7

SUCCESS – WHAT DOES IT REALLY MEAN TO YOU?

The Meaning of Life is to find your gift; The Purpose of Life is to give it away. ~ **Unknown**

The poem "One Flaw in Women" is so affirming because it reminds me how beautiful, strong, wise, and incredible we as women are. Whenever you know of a women struggling with their self-worth, please send them this poem! Without a woman knowing her full self-worth, it is impossible to reach her full potential and be successful.

As women, we have unrealistic expectations of ourselves that will set us up for failure if we try to meet "society's expectations." In the book "Successful Women Think Differently" by Valerie Burton she states "statistics show men are happier than women and with age, men tend to get happier, whereas women tend to get more depressed after the age of 40." I think you will agree women feel more pressure than men. For example, if someone comes over to your house and the house is nasty and children are misbehaving, who normally gets the finger pointed at them? The woman.

It is important that women <u>define the real fulfillment of life for themselves</u>. What things really matter to you in life? Author Burton talks about considering these five ways to define success:

1. Value fulfillment more than success – success in our culture is often defined by the external – money, job, titles, and possessions. Fulfillment is about living with purpose.

2. Aim for excellence not success – If you aim for the moment, aiming to be your best, success will follow. Success is about the journey, not the destination.

3. Measure your success by your own, not society's. Consider the five key areas of your life – relationships, work, finances, health, and spirituality.

4. Ask "What's my impact?" One indicator of success is making a positive difference in the world. Serving in some way is the greatest thing we can do.

5. Ask "Is my success making me a better person?" Are you bitter or better when faced with adversity?

6. Be patient. Know that delay is not denial. Know that God will release the blessing in due time and when He does… it will be worth the wait.

Once we realize the true meaning of success for ourselves, we can begin to create our own definition of success rather than trying to live up to society's definition of success as women. Times have changed. Women now bring home the bacon and play a major role in the household, but there has to be a balance. We will talk more about this in the next chapter.

Success will have a different meaning to different people. One person may say "Success means accomplishing goals I have set." Another may say "Success is forming goals no matter how big or small." For each person, it will be different. The key factor is to define your own goal so that society does not define it for you.

My definition of success is "Setting goals and actively working to achieve those goals I have set in the areas of family, faith, finances, career, and fitness." My purpose and vision aligns with this definition of success. Everything I consider valuable and important falls into these areas. Serve – faith. Children and marriage – Family. Health – Fitness. Preparing for the future and leaving a legacy for my children – Finances. This is my definition of success. What's yours?

Give and Empower Others

"The best way to not feel hopeless is to get up and do something. Don't wait for good things to happen to you. If you go out and make things happen for others you will fill the world with hope and in return you will fill yourself with hope". ~ Barak Obama

"A kind gesture can reach a wound that only compassion can heal." ~ Unknown

Once you have reached a certain level of success, it is important to inspire others to do the same. When you see someone struggling in the same area you have struggled and overcome, lend a helping hand to help them get on the right track. Be transparent. Be willing to share your failures as well as your successes. Explain the steps you took to overcome. Listen to them, challenge them, encourage them, and mentor them. Remember, you can't give them the formula for their own success, but you can share some of the trials you went through to prevent them from making some of the same mistakes you made.

I know a big amount of my success is that I am a good listener. Even when people don't think I'm listening and looking, I am. Some mistakes I made because I didn't listen and some mistakes I didn't make because I did listen. I saw some of the struggles people before me endured as a teen mother. As a result, I knew I didn't want to go down that path. I heard some of the stories of people who have stayed in abusive relationships which is why it only took someone to hit me one time and I was gone. I saw the effects of people who have tried crack and cocaine which is why I haven't ever tried that. I attended School of Marriage by Apostle Ricky and Sheila Floyd and listened to some of the trials they endured in marriage. Consequently, we overcame some of those trials listening to their stories and hearing the principles they applied to overcome. Listening is powerful. Sharing is powerful. Inspiration is powerful and a necessity.

I told my husband, "Sometimes we give the devil too much power." Every problem that occurred in our life is not the devil. Sometimes it's us. Sometimes we refused to listen and apply the principles people shared with us. As a result, we got in certain situations and then we had to apply the principles to get out of them.

Remember, thriving is not all about you. Jesus said in his Word the two greatest commandments are "To Love the Lord Your God with all your heart, soul, and mind and to love your neighbor as yourself." If it was all about you, He would've said, "Love yourself to the fullest." Statistics show people who give back are happier, healthier and live longer and guess who else is happy? GOD!

God put this book on my heart because if I continue to hold all the experiences I've gone through and I am not using my story to encourage others, what was the purpose of the struggles? I went through those experiences for a reason and you did, too. You need to have a way to share your story. God put it on my heart to write a book, but He may lead you to do something else. The important factor is to share your story to help and empower others.

I encourage you to find an area that you are passionate in and seek ways you can help. For example, if you are passionate about education and youth, research organizations such as 5 for 5 or my husband's organization 3 V Leader and find a way to help whether it be monetary or volunteering your time. If you are passionate about single mothers, research organizations that help single mothers and find a way to help them. I guarantee you will be blessed and happier by doing so.

Thriving Tools:

1. Define success for yourself so you don't feel the pressure to live up to society's definition of success.

2. Consider the things that really matter to you in life. The areas that bring fulfillment to your life.

3. Ask yourself, is your success making you a better person and if not, think of ways it can.

4. Once you have overcome, share your story. Be authentic. Be transparent and inspire others.

Thriving Points to Consider:

What is your definition of success?

How does your definition of success align with your purpose and vision?

What are your areas of fulfillment in life?

Is success making you a better person or a bitter person? Why?

Will your success inspire others? How?

Thriving Additional Resources:

- Book – Valerie Burton - *Successful Women Think Differently*

Thriving Prayer:

God, I thank you for opening my eyes to what success really means. Help me to walk into success as a person who is better and not bitter. Help me to live up to my definition of success and not society's. I know that success can sometimes lead to pride and arrogance, but help me to stay humble in the process. I thank you that while I am successful, I will have the gifts of the spirit – love, joy, peace, patience, kindness, goodness, faithfulness, gentleness, and self-control. In Jesus' Name. Amen.

Thriving Confession:

I am successful and I walk it out every day. I display love, joy, peace, patience, kindness, goodness, faithfulness, gentleness, and self-control. I am stronger and wiser in the areas that fulfill my life. Everyone who I cross paths with is a greater person because I am successful and I have impacted their life in a positive way. In Jesus' Name! Amen.

These Things I Have

I wanted health and strength to do great things,
Infirmity taught patience for each day.
My strength, as fleeting as a moth's white wing,
Left me dependent, that I might obey.

I wanted wealth for happiness and ease,
But poverty prevailed and made me wise.
I wanted power to conquer and to please,
But weakness made me see through others' eyes.

I wanted leisure time to dream and plan,
But duty brought self-discipline, and while
I sought approval of my fellowman,
I found it not, but in my Savior's smile.

And now that I have been so richly blest,
This is my daily prayer, "Give what is best."

~ **Uknown**

CHAPTER 8
BALANCING WHILE THRIVING

My husband and I get asked often, "How do you guys do all that you do with six children?" The answer is we complement each other well. We have a system in place. Often times, I look through our calendar and think "How did we do all that last month?" but we do it and we do it well. Our children are doing well in school; two headed off to college and others are excelling in their academics. Our house is not spiffy clean, but it's clean and I keep it organized. We know how to balance.

Seek Help From Others

I don't let society's expectations put me in a position where I overextend myself. For example, when I worked 8-5 I wasn't in a position to pop up at our children's schools, but my husband does it often. At any moment, our children know Dad can pop up and he will when they least expect him to. Also, I know he has many community events to attend to on Saturdays, so I try to prevent from scheduling any meetings on that day to allow him to do what he needs to do. We have a system. We use Google calendar. We both put our appointments in this calendar so we can schedule accordingly.

We also rely heavily on our older children. We have the expectation of them to do things around the house and help out with their little sisters and brothers. For that contribution, we pay them a weekly allowance. This takes the pressure off of us and also teaches them responsibility at a young age. We also have the help of other family members and friends. We will keep their children sometimes and in return they will keep all of ours. This time allows us to do things we need to get done while they are gone.

Know Your Balance

It is important to know your balance. I know when I've had enough. I know my limits. I work hard, plan hard, but I also work smart. I know my body needs one day a week to just unwind. This day is normally Saturday or Sunday for me. A day where I can do whatever I want to do – sit in the bed and watch Lifetime all day or read a book, or go get a mani and pedi. I know my body limits and I know what it needs. Each person may be different, but it is important to know what your balance is.

Eliminate the Feeling of Guilt

It is important to not put any guilt on yourself for working outside the home. Replace that negative thought with a positive thought saying, "Because I have a career with a steady income my children are able to enjoy the lifestyle they have." If you are not there yet, then look at the lifestyle they WILL be able to enjoy because of the steady income you will be bringing in. It is important, once your children reach the age where they can understand, you sit them down and talk to them about the expectations and responsibilities of the job. This will help them to understand that mommy is doing this because she wants a better life for them and also will help them to understand responsibility.

For example, our children know that Dad does a lot of work in the community to help other children who don't have all that they have. This also puts the attitude of service in them at a young age. We express to them, "You walking around here with your iPad and iPhone and there are children out there who have to go home to a house with no electricity and no food."

Use Technology

There are advantages and disadvantages for having email come directly to your phone but the key is in balance. I do have email come directly to my phone, but a lot of times I don't respond to emails until I am at work the next day. I only read through my emails at night so I can get a mental checklist of what I need to do the next day. I know I am not at my peak at night so I don't even try to respond to emails at night. Some people prefer not to check their emails after hours depending on the demand of their job. Some jobs require you to check your emails regularly. Know the demand and expectation of your job when you are interviewing if you are not in that position. If you are in that position, just do the best you can do and leave the rest up to God.

Prioritize Accordingly

When given an assignment, always ask your deadline date. This will help you to prioritize your time wisely to try to prevent from doing work at home. If an assignment will require work at home, express that to your children and husband (if applicable) and let them know this is another expectation that mommy has to meet. Then, try to do something to spend more time with them. Rather than cooking, pick up some food to give you that little extra time to spend with the kids.

Again, set your own balance. Don't let society's expectations say you have to cook every night when you have a partner or children who are old enough to cook. Choose your time wisely and remember to not over extend yourself to the point of exhaustion. Know that you don't have to be perfect. Strive for excellence and rest at night knowing you did your best and will do your best the next day.

Thriving Tools:

> **1.** Eliminate society's roles of how you should be a good mother and make up your own.
>
> **2.** Seek help from others if you can. Engage your children and spouse to help. Don't try to do it all by yourself.
>
> **3.** Know your balance. If you don't have that time for just you to unwind, you are no good to your family or career.
>
> **4.** Eliminate the feeling or thought of guilt and replace it with a positive thought or feeling.
>
> **5.** Prioritize accordingly. Know your deadline dates and use your time wisely.

CONCLUSION

I hope this book has inspired and provided you with tools to THRIVE. Again, I don't want you to think that I have it altogether, but I do know I have come a long way from where I was 10 years ago to where I am today. I wanted to share with you some of the knowledge I have gained and steps I have taken along the way. Remember, start where you are and have a plan in place to get where you want to be.

You can THRIVE where you are while STRIVING to get where you want in every area of your life. There is nothing stopping you from thriving but *you.* No obstacle or barrier is preventing you from climbing to the top. God has placed immeasurable potential within you. It is up to you to operate in immeasurable faith to obtain it. Be tenacious, go through the healing process. Reflect where you are and where you want to be. Use your imagination to think of creative ways to change your current situation. Write the vision and make it plain. Engage with people who will support you and eliminate those that won't. THRIVE TO THE TOP AND SERVE GOD'S PEOPLE ALONG THE WAY.

Honor God by developing your potential with determination and persistence. Don't allow anything to interfere with your commitment.

ABOUT THE AUTHOR

Teresa Landrum Caswell is a native of Decatur, Illinois. She moved to Memphis, TN as a single mother on welfare that went through many obstacles to mold her into the woman she is today. While serving under the leadership of Apostle Ricky and Sheila Floyd at the Pursuit of God Transformation Center, she met her husband Charlie Caswell. Teresa is now happily married for 8 years and has 6 beautiful children in a blended family.

Teresa has a Masters Degree in Business Administration. In addition, she has her insurance license in Life and Health where she is a representative of Primerica. As an entrepreneur, Teresa has her own consulting business, TLC Consulting, where she provides career development to individuals and administration to businesses.

Teresa loves to serve others. Her favorite motto is: "The best way to serve God is to serve God's people" by Rick Warren. She and her husband serve the community in a variety of ways. They were featured in 2011 on the National Geographic Channel for hosting a Father Daughter Purity Ball where 30 teenage girls made a vow to remain pure until marriage. Teresa believes this is instrumental in imbedding the value of "purity" for women at a young age because she also was in a purity ball at the age of 16.

In her spare time, Teresa loves to read romance novels and inspirational books. She also loves to listen to music. She has recently experienced her first cruise and now has taken this on as a new passion as well.

Teresa owes a huge amount of her success to her upbringing – she gets her drive and ambition from her father, Aljay Landrum, and her compassion from her mother, Lula Landrum. Teresa has one sister (Tamika Landrum) two brothers – one deceased (James Dennis) and Jason Landrum who have always looked out for her as the "baby" of the family. She highly respects all of her siblings knowing that they all encourage, motivate, and challenge each other, including herself, to be a better person.

For more information, email: landrum.tlcconsulting@gmail.com

REFERENCES

Angelou, Mayo. *Phenomenal Woman.* 5 May 2015. Poem.

Caswell, Charlie A., Jr. "How to Become Visible, Vocal, and Valuable to Your Community." 2013.

Covey, Stephen R. *The 7 Habits of Highly Effective People.* London: Simon & Schuster, 2005.

Deci, Edward L., and Richard Flaste. *Why We Do What We Do: Understanding Self-motivation.* New York: Penguins, 1996.

Facing the Giants. 10 My 2015. Movie.

"Famous Quotes." *BrainyQuote.* Xplore, n.d. Web. 15 May 2015.

"Famous Quotes" Bainyquote. *If you Fail.* 15 May 2015.

Fireproof. 5 May 2015. Movie.

Godvine.com. 10 May 2015. Image.

Houghton, Israel, Chevelle Franklyn, Martin Smith, Tommy Sims, and Tobymac. *The Power of One.* Integrity Music, 2009. CD.

Kiyosaki, Robert T., and Sharon L. Lechter. *Rich Dad, Poor Dad: What the Rich Teach Their Kids about Money-- That the Poor and Middle Class Do Not!* New York: Warner Business, 2000.

Maxwell, John C. *Developing the Leader within You.* Nashville: T. Nelson, 1993.

Meyer, Joyce. *Battlefield of the Mind: Winning the Battle in Your Mind*. New York, NY: Warner, 2002.

Munroe, Myles. *The Principles and Power of Vision*. New Kensington, PA: Whitaker House, 2003.

"Poetry Daily, a New Poem Every Day." *Poetry Daily, a New Poem Every Day*. N.p., n.d. Web. 10 May 2015.

"Rhyming Poems." *Anita Poems*. N.p., n.d. Web. 10 May 2015.

"Rhyming Poems." Lucky Zwane

Shivley, Lydia. *The Things I Have*. 15 May 2015. Poem.

The Pursuit of Happyness. 15 May 2015. Movie.

The Secret. 15 May 2015. Movie.

"Online Dictionary." *Webster Dictionary*. N.p., n.d. Web. 10 May 2015.

Warren, Richard. *The Purpose-driven Life: What on Earth Am I Here For?* Grand Rapids, MI: Zondervan, 2002.

You Aren't Meant to Just Survive in Life. You Are Meant to Thrive. There IS a Higher Purpose. Digital image. Fb.com.rochellegriffinfitness, n.d. Web. 5 Mar. 2015.

Zwane, Lucky. *The Mind Is the Battle Ground*. 10 May 2015. Poem.

APPENDIX

ENTREPRENEURSHIP is living a few years of your life like most people won't so that you can spend the rest of your life like most people can't.

~ **A student in Warren G. Tracy's class, entrepreneur**

Failure defeats losers, failure inspires winners.
Robert T. Kiyosaki, author, entrepreneur, investor

Multi-Level Marketing – Advantages and Disadvantages

Remember, we are looking at things from a different lens. Why do you have that perception on MLM? Maybe because it didn't work for one person or maybe because it didn't work for you the first time, but what about all the other people it did work for? Maybe you didn't put enough time and effort into it? When your previous job didn't work out, did you stop working or did you try something different? If it is our desire to be wealthy and leave a legacy for our children and grandchildren…do you see that happening with a 8-5 job?

MLM is not for everyone, but I want you to see things from a different lens to get different results. As I tell people about my business I am involved in, it costs $99 to get started. Therefore, even if it doesn't work what did you lose and if it does work what did you gain? Do your research of the company. What is their rating with BBB? How long has the business been operating? Who do you know that is successful? What does the compensation offer?

I encourage you to read the book "Rich Dad Poor Dad" by Robert Kiyosaki. This will change your lens on MLM. Author Kiyosaki talks about the two main reasons to invest in MLM:

1. To help yourself – change from Employee to Investor and Entrepreneur
2. To help others – while you are investing in yourself you are also investing in others

The Rich Don't Work for Money ~ Robert Kiyosaki

MLM has many advantages:

- *Small amount of risk or investment*
- *Unlimited income potential:* With MLM you get what you put into it. The sky is the limit. Can you say that about your 8-5 job?
- *Low operating cost:* You are a business owner with little or no overhead. You don't have to worry about light bill, rent, inventory, etc.
- *The attainable freedom:* You work your hours at your time. You don't have to punch a clock nor do you have to get permission from your boss to take off.
- *You make $ in your sleep:* Guess what… you can be asleep and be making money from your downline. Tell me, do you have that benefit on your 8-5?
- *Entrepreneur:* You are the business owner so you get the opportunity to write business expenses off on your taxes. You will receive a 1099.

Some common myths about MLM:

- *"MLM is a scam":* This is what a lot of people believe because of how it is sold. People tell you, "You can make a lot of money with little or no effort." That is a lie. Anytime you hear that you run. Yes, you can make a lot of $ but you will have to put in the effort. Anything that is given freely is not appreciated. With MLM you get what you put in it.
- *"I'm terrible at marketing and I don't want to bother my friends and family with this":* You can think like that or you can think like this "I see an opportunity to leave a legacy and I want to share this opportunity with my friends and family." For some people, you will have to take on the mindset of "I can show you better than I can tell you."

- Career Portfolios – Cover Letter, Resumes, and References
- Interview Tips
- Administration – Budgeting, Organizing, and Data Entry
- Computer Training – Microsoft Office Suites
- Data Entry

http://caswell-28.wix.com/tlcconsulting

Check out Charlie Caswell's (Teresa Landrum-Caswell's husband) book
How to Become More Visible, Vocal, and Valuable:

Elder Charlie Caswell, Jr. is a husband, father, outreach pastor, community activist, entrepreneur, author, and great man of vision. Elder Caswell was born and raised in the projects of Dixie Homes in Memphis, TN. Elder

Caswell is truly a man after God's own heart. He has dedicated all of his adulthood to being a community activist in the city of Memphis and Atlanta, GA. Elder Caswell serves as a community activist that provides his 3V Leader curriculum to an after school and parent training program for stakeholders in his community. He is CEO of 3V Leader, a radio personality on AM730 Memphis in the Morning, and former Executive Director of Rangeline Neighborhood Community Development Corporation, a non-profit with a focus of "Putting the Neighbor Back in the Hood." He is an Elder with The Pursuit of God Church in Frayser. Elder Caswell is the author of his first book "How to Become More Visible, Vocal, and Valuable to your Community." It is a book based on the work he has done as a community leader.

     Elder Caswell owes a lot of his successes to a good upbringing and the mentorship of many great men in his life such as Director Toney Armstrong, Pastor Ricky Floyd and Pastor Walter Smith.

     Elder Caswell is the proud father of 6 beautiful children and the husband of Mrs. Teresa Landrum Caswell.

For more information, email 3vleader@gmail.com or go to www.caswell-28.wix.com/3VLeader

Annie's Scale Back

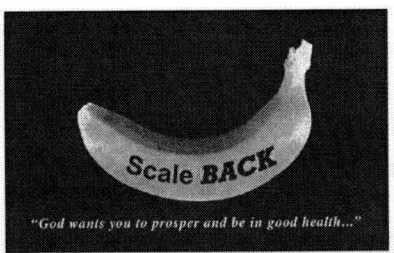

Vision

The vision of Scale Back is to promote healthy living through lifestyle changes including nutrition and exercise. This lifestyle change will cultivate a positive attitude for others preventing life threatening diseases caused by obesity and lack of knowledge of proper nutrition.

Mission

The mission of Scale Back is to motivate individuals in getting healthy by changing bad eating habits and promoting daily exercise.

For more information, go to http://scaleback6182011.wix.com/health

Before **Now (After Losing 80 lbs.)**